DESIGN YOUR LIFE

Design Thinking ○ Positive Psychology
Practical Spirituality

Akhilesh N Singh

Design Your Life Coach
Management Consultant

NewDelhi • London

BLUEROSE PUBLISHERS
India | U.K.

Copyright © Akhilesh N Singh 2024

All rights reserved by author. No part of this publication may be reproduced, stored in a retrieval system or transmitted in any form or by any means, electronic, mechanical, photocopying, recording or otherwise, without the prior permission of the author. Although every precaution has been taken to verify the accuracy of the information contained herein, the publisher assume no responsibility for any errors or omissions. No liability is assumed for damages that may result from the use of information contained within.

BlueRose Publishers takes no responsibility for any damages, losses, or liabilities that may arise from the use or misuse of the information, products, or services provided in this publication.

For permissions requests or inquiries regarding this publication, please contact:

BLUEROSE PUBLISHERS
www.BlueRoseONE.com
info@bluerosepublishers.com
+91 8882 898 898
+4407342408967

ISBN: 978-93-6261-506-0

Cover design: Tahira
Typesetting: Tanya Raj Upadhyay

First Edition: August 2024

Foreword

Everyone is born to live a life in this world. The quality of an individual's life depends on the choice one makes; either life "by default" – governed by circumstances, or "by design"- as per own dreams and aspirations?

Most people are living life by default, mainly driven by work life. Despite attaining great success in the profession, they live unfulfilled life. To live a holistic life one wish to live in the future, needs to be designed. But how to design life- is a big challenge and this is an innovative initiative taken by the author.

The design of life begins with an understanding of three fundamental questions: what is life all about? what is the purpose of life? and, how to accomplish this very purpose?

Even modern medical science and Google can't give true answers. It comes through satisfying esteem needs and to an extent by way of self-actualization. Of course, the true answer can be found in our ancient Vedas- the source of ultimate knowledge.

The author Akhilesh Singh, a quality professional, and author of several books, has been actively associated with me in several quality initiatives during my tenure as Secretary General-Quality Council of India, and currently as Director General- Association of Healthcare Providers India.

He has constantly been pursuing study of Vedanta and spirituality along with learning TQM. By synergizing the principles of quality and spirituality, he has attempted to expand his horizon of activities from improving the quality of objects to the quality of the subject- human life.

During my five decades in the quality profession, I observed that the quality of products has significantly improved, resulting in the financial growth of organizations and people. However, the quality of people's lives is deteriorating, especially in areas including; physical health, mental peace, environment, and overall happiness. I believe modern technology can't design solutions. Every individual has to design their life.

A practical framework "design your life" presented in the book is a unique combination of practical spirituality, positive psychology, and design thinking. It has nicely synergized the Western concepts of modern management with the Eastern eternal wisdom of Vedas and spirituality.

In addition to helping the professionals to design their lives, this book will help them to bring up their children with higher values and positive thinking to live a happy life.

I hope this book serves its purpose of facilitating readers to design a life they wish to live.

Dr. Girdhar Gyani
Director General, Association of Healthcare Providers India
Former Secretary General, Quality Council of India,

Preface

Incidentally, I am actively associated with quality management discipline for over five decades as an engineer, academician, quality management practitioner, consultant, corporate trainer, auditor, and author. Got excellent opportunities to learn latest operational excellence techniques in global leading companies of Japan, United States, United Kingdom, and many other countries. Along with my engineering and quality management education and learning, I pursued my passion in field of spirituality and tried to learn and study Vedantic scriptures including; Upanishads, Yoga Sutra, Brahma Sutra, Bhagavad-Gita, Yoga Vasishta, Vedic Jyotish, etc. from realized Gurus. In addition to quality management and spirituality, I tried to learn the western concepts of positive psychology, neuro linguistic programming, mind management and design thinking also.

Based on my direct experiences of quality management, and practice of spirituality, I inferred that quality management is focusing on improving the quality of objects used by the people, whereas spirituality focuses on improving quality of life of people by inner transformation, which is rather more important.

During the last five decades of my professional career, I observed tremendous developments in quality of products and services along with economic growth of organizations and people, but overall health, relationships, inner peace, and happiness of people have drastically deteriorated. I hope you will agree with my observation that *"beyond a point, materialistic success is inversely proportional to happiness".*

If we reflect on the causes of deterioration in quality of life, one of the main causes is "materialism" and myth that money is most important in life. Whether it is a teen ager- who prefers a course that gives highest salary, a professional- measures annual package, an industrialist or corporate leader always busy in making strategies to maximize profit, and a country head talks about trillions dollar economy. The purpose of life of every person is to earn maximum wealth, without knowing what for, and how much? No doubt money gives some financial freedom to get luxurious objects, but increases ego of people, that is the worst effect of money.

The creator of universe is the greatest designer. According to natural design everyone is born with a set of four personality constituents; body-mind-intellect-spirit, and lives in four domains of life; physical, family, work, and spiritual. As per Vedic wisdom, the purpose of everyone's life is to seek happiness. But due to ignorance, majority of people are mainly focusing on work domain of life to attain career success and create plenty of wealth, even at the cost of physical, family and spiritual lives. Based on my exposure of scriptures, I believe without spiritual knowledge, awareness, and practice of yoga and meditation, no one can attain inner peace and true happiness in life, despite creating plenty of wealth and great success in career.

Positive psychology is a relatively new branch of psychology evolved as science of happiness, defines it as combination of subjective wellbeing and positive emotions. Vedic scriptures describe happiness as natural characteristics of soul, revealed when one is with oneself. In fact, happiness is a true and natural need of every person. Happiness cannot come by itself, you have to "Design Your Life" and live according to your aspirations to experience true happiness.

In this book effort has been made to synergize three most relevant techniques; positive psychology, practical spirituality, and design thinking. Positive psychology focuses on development of positive emotions, practical spirituality explains how to connect with inner self- the real source of happiness, and design thinking is a human centered problem-solving technique, which can be used to solve life problems.

In this book a unique "sailboat metaphor" is used to translate life philosophy into practically implementable steps to attain the purpose of life. According to sailboat metaphor, human life is like a sailboat, on a lifelong journey in a sea of physical world, just like sailboat, life can be also steered in right direction towards a meaningful destination to attain the purpose of life. By identifying and mending the personal weaknesses (like the leaks in the sailboat) that hinder progress and by enhancing personal strengths one can solve the problems of life and make a successful journey with higher purpose in lesser time. Sailboat metaphor developed by positive psychology institute is modified by introducing spiritual dimension to make it holistic.

This book is collection of ideas, thoughts, and techniques to improve quality of life, picked up from the teachings of several learned Gurus, authors, and experts of Vedanta, Positive Psychology, and Design Thinking.

The purpose of this book is to create awareness and applicability of spiritual concepts along with positive psychology not only to present generation of professionals, but to inspire them cultivate divine "samskaras" (good values and behavior) in their children. It is moral responsibility of every person to pass on a better world, good environment, righteous values, and happy life to our next generation. This can be made possible, only by learning and practicing spirituality and positive psychology principles in everyday life.

I hope, this book will be able to serve its purpose and help the professionals to design their life to improve all four domains of life; physical (health), family (emotional), work (intellectual), and spiritual (inner peace).

Finally, I am grateful to all readers who have found it worth reading and adopting the concepts to design their lives. I will be delighted to receive readers' comments about contents, utility, quality, and deficiencies of the book. (ansingh11@gmail.com)

1st August 2024   Akhilesh N Singh

Table of Contents

Chapter 1: The Need 1

Chapter 2: Demystifying Life 13

Chapter 3: The Sailboat Metaphor 36

Chapter 4: Life You Wish To Live 55

Chapter 5: Design Your Life 63

Chapter 6: Self-Discovery 71

Chapter 7: Direction & Destination Of Life 83

Chapter 8: Personal Weaknesses & Strengths 103

Chapter 9: Challenges & Staying Aligned 140

Chapter 10
Weathers & People Around 162

Chapter 11: Take Control Of Your Destiny 171

Chapter 12: Steering Towards Tomorrow 182

Acknowledgments 196

About The Author 198

Design Your Life: Two-Day In-House Workshop 200

Chapter 1
The Need

The human beings, including you and me, are the crown of creation. The supreme creator, a perfect designer has designed every person with a purpose. The purpose is the cause of creation and existence of any entity. Due to ignorance of the purpose of life, many people take a wrong path, and finally they suffer and regret. Do you know the purpose of your life? Probably no! This is the most important need of every person to discover the purpose of life, and design a life one wish to live.

Deep down, we all crave for a life that feels fulfilling and successful. It's a universal human desire, regardless of background, culture, or current circumstances. Yet, translating the desire into reality is one of the greatest challenges of everyone's life. The purpose of this book is to facilitate you to know the purpose of life, and design a successful and fulfilling life.

Let us analyze the life story of some professionally successful people, who could not live fulfilling life, and explore how to live a truly happy and successful life.

1.1 Robin: A Corporate Professional

Robin, a graduate in humanities joined a leading metal manufacturing company as an office assistant, due to his sincerity and talent he became an HR manager in a few years, and grown to the position of Director of Human Resources

and finally the CEO of the company. He was recognized as a brilliant corporate leader and an excellent man manager. But, due to some personal conflicts, he could not maintain a good relationship with his spouse. His lifestyle was mainly work-focused, no adequate time for family and any spiritual development. He lived his life, driven by external circumstances, and never did any introspection and life planning. As a CEO he took few decisions against the policies of the company, even after several warnings by the management, finally, he was removed from his services by the board of directors. Despite a successful career and economic prosperity, he could not live a happy and fulfilling life. Now let's analyze the life story of Robin, and find out the reasons for his unhappy life:

Robin's Strengths: Robin's career trajectory shows that he was a hardworking and dedicated person, who was able to rise through the ranks of the company. Good people manager, which suggests he has strong interpersonal skills.

Robin's Shortcomings: Lack of self-awareness- Robin seems to have been unaware of the impact of his work-centric lifestyle on his personal life. Poor work-life balance- Robin prioritized work over his family and personal well-being. Robin made ego-driven decisions that went against company policy, despite warnings. This suggests that he may have been resistant to feedback.

Robin could have lived a happier and more meaningful life by practicing the following activities:

- **Self-reflection:** Robin could have benefited from spending time on introspection to identify his values and what was truly important to him in life.
- **Goal setting:** Setting goals in all areas of life that included personal and professional development would have given Robin a more balanced perspective.
- **Work-life balance:** Robin needed to find a way to manage his work hours in a way that allowed him to spend time with his family and pursue personal interests.
- **Communication:** Open and honest communication with his spouse could have helped Robin maintain a good relationship.
- **Design Your Life:** Robin should have lived his life "by design" instead of the current way of living "by default".

Robin's story highlights the fact that even the most successful people can fall on hard times, if they don't take the time to design their lives. When we design our lives, we take control of our destinies. We set goals, identify our values, and make choices that will help us achieve the life we want.

1.2 Evengela: A Banker

Evengela, joined as a management trainee in a leading bank, due to her exceptional talent and leadership qualities, she reached on the top position as CEO of the bank. She established several benchmarks for the banking sector and received many prestigious national and international awards for her extraordinary achievements. She was focused on maximizing the profits of the bank. She did not have any time

to learn meditate and connect with her inner self. However, her career came to a crashing halt when it was revealed that she had approved a large loan that did not meet the bank's requirements and questioned her integrity. This loan subsequently became a bad debt, causing significant financial losses to the bank. Evengela was removed from her position and faced legal proceedings. Financially she had a successful career and created plenty of wealth from her salary, but now living a distressful life.

Analysis of Evengela's life story: Her life story highlights the importance of "design your life". By taking a more thoughtful approach to her career path, she might have avoided the mistakes that led to her downfall. Here's what the Evengela could have done to live a happier life:

- **Clarifying her values:** If Evengela had taken the time to identify her core values, she might have been more likely to question the loan approval process. Perhaps her values would have emphasized honesty and integrity, which could have prevented her from approving a loan that she knew did not meet the bank's standards.

- **Setting goals:** Setting clear goals for her career would have given Evengela a roadmap to follow. These goals could have included not only achieving financial success but also maintaining high ethical standards.

- **Identifying her strengths and weaknesses:** A self-assessment could have helped Evengela identify any areas where she was particularly vulnerable to making mistakes. For example, perhaps she was overly trusting of others or had a blind spot for ethical considerations.

- **Balance work and personal life:** Evengela "Did not have any time to learn and meditate and to connect with her inner self." It seems like she was so focused on work that she neglected other parts of her life that could have brought her happiness.

- **Find purpose beyond work:** Even though Evengela was successful in her career, she is now living a "distressful life". This suggests that her work did not provide her with a sense of purpose in life.

Overall, designing a happy life is about finding a balance that works for you. It's about achieving success in your field but also prioritizing your well-being and making choices that you can be proud of.

1.3 Rocky: An Actor

Rocky, joined as a business executive of a marketing company. Due to his passion for theatre and drama, after a few years, he left the corporate job to pursue his interests in the film industry. After struggling for some time, he got a small role in a film, and his acting performance attracted the film producers. Due to his acting talent and unique dialogue delivery, finally he got lead roles in many box-office successful films and became a superstar. He attained great success in his career, created plenty of wealth, and obtained many national and international awards. However, due to some lifestyle problems, strained relationships, and health issues he could not live a truly fulfilled

life. Despite being a superstar, celebrity, and a wealthy person, he is living an unhappy and lonely life.

Rocky's story illustrates how even achieving your dreams, it will leave you feeling empty, if you haven't considered what truly matters to you in life. Here's how designing the life could have helped Rocky:

- **Considering long-term goals:** Rocky pursued his passion for film but did not have clear goals beyond just becoming a celebrity. Designing his life could have helped him identify what he wanted to achieve with his success, such as using his platform to make a positive impact or create a lasting legacy.

- **Building a support system:** Rocky had strained relationships with his close family members. Designing his life could have prompted him to consider the importance of building a strong support system of family, friends, and mentors who could provide guidance and emotional support throughout his career.

- **Maintaining a work-life balance:** Because of highly busy shooting schedules, he could not pay attention to his health, family, and relationships. Designing his life could have helped him establish a healthy work-life balance to avoid neglecting his well-being in the pursuit of professional success.

1.4 Jacob: An IT Professional

Jacob, an IT professional and entrepreneur started a software company and developed some most useful software. Being one of the pioneering software companies he established one of the most successful IT organizations. Due to his materialistic mindset, competitive spirit, and ambition to remain as the topmost company, he ignored his physical, family and spiritual domains of life. Despite attaining great success in his career and business, Jacob could not maintain a cordial relationship with his wife, and even after many years of companionship finally, Jacob and his spouse opted for breakup. After such an eventful life, now they are living lonely lives. To escape from loneliness, he took an initiative to improve quality of life of poor people, and keeping himself busy with several social works.

Based on analysis of Jacob's life story, here is why he could not attain real fulfillment in life:

- **Prioritizing the material success:** Jacob prioritized material success and professional achievement over spiritual and other aspects of life. Designing his life could have helped him identify a wider range of values, well-being, relationships, and personal growth.

- **Ignoring Work-Life Balance:** Jacob's focus on work seems to have negatively impacted his marriage. Designing his life could have helped him establish boundaries and create a healthier work-life balance.

- **Lack of Self-Awareness:** Jacob does not have spiritual knowledge and awareness. Designing his life could have prompted him to explore his values, motivations, and what truly brings him fulfillment.

- **Design your life:** Jacob's focus was mainly on building a successful company. Designing his life could have prompted him to consider the importance of nurturing his relationship with his wife. It could have helped him establish boundaries between his work life and personal life.

As described in brief case studies of Robin, Evengela, Rocky, and Jacob, there are plenty of such real characters around you in society, who are professionally brilliant, attained great success in their career, created plenty of wealth, and have all luxurious objects of desire. But, despite of great success in their career, they don't have inner peace and true happiness. Why?

- Probably, they don't know themselves?
- They don't know their core values?
- They don't know whether their life is in right or wrong direction?
- They didn't design their life and living a partial life.
- Probably, they believe happiness is directly proportional to materialistic success

1.5 Materialistic Success and Happiness

This is a myth that materialistic success is proportional to happiness. Happiness and materialistic success have a complex relationship, but not directly proportional. Here's a breakdown:

- **Limited Correlation:** Studies suggest a correlation between income and happiness, but only up to a certain point (around $75,000 annually in some studies of USA). Beyond that, more money doesn't necessarily lead to more happiness.

- **Mindset Matters:** Focusing on material possessions as the key to happiness (happiness materialism) can actually backfire, leading to dissatisfaction and a feeling of needing more. However, viewing success as a way to improve your life (success materialism) can be motivating and contribute to happiness.
- **Other Factors Play a Role:** Strong relationships, good health, meaningful work, spirituality and personal growth all contribute to happiness more than just material wealth.

Overall, materialistic success can be a tool to achieve a better life, but it's not a guarantee of happiness. Focusing on intrinsic factors and a balanced life is more important for long-term happiness

In conclusion, professionals need an innovative and practical approach to design and live life that can help them to understand themselves and their life vision. Discover their personal values, facilitate to determine right direction and destination, mend their weaknesses and develop strengths to navigate the journey to a more fulfilling and successful life, both personally and professionally.

1.6 Understanding Your Current Life

Everyone's is living life either "by default" or "by design". How about you? Check the type of life you are living:

Life by Default:

- This means going with the flow passively, letting life happen to you instead of actively shaping it.

- You might fall into routines or jobs without much thought, or simply react to situations instead of planning ahead.
- It can feel comfortable in the short term, but can lead to a lack of fulfilment and feeling stuck.

Life by Design:

- This is about taking an active role in crafting the life you want.
- You set goals, make choices that align with your values, and take steps to get where you want to be.
- It requires intentionality and effort, but can lead to a greater sense of purpose and happiness.

Here is an analogy: Imagine you are in a sailboat, floating in the vast ocean. Living life by default means; your sailboat is moving in any direction depending on the wind velocity and direction, you don't have any control on it. But, when you are living life by design, you are adjusting your sails and steering your sailboat to move towards the desired destination.

1.7 Pursuing Your Ideal Life

To live a life of your aspirations, you have to design your life. The "Design Your Life" is a philosophy that empowers you to take control of your life and create a future that is both fulfilling and successful. Through a process of self-discovery and exploration, you will gain a deep understanding of your values, strengths, and passions. This knowledge will serve as a compass, guiding you toward a life that is aligned with your deepest desires and values. Here are some of the benefits of Design Your Life:

- **Living a holistic life:** As per the divine design, everyone is born with four natural constituents of personality; body, mind, intellect, and spirit. Accordingly, people have four domains of life: physical life, emotional (family) life, intellectual (work) life, and spiritual life. To attain happiness all four domains must be addressed and lived. But the majority of people are focusing on two or three domains, live a partial and incomplete life. By designing your life, you will live a holistic life in all four natural domains.

  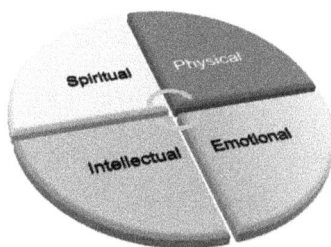

  Four domains of Holistic Life

- **Clarity and Focus:** Design Your Life will help you to identify your core values and goals. With this newfound clarity, you can make decisions that are in line with what is truly important to you.

- **Greater Happiness and Fulfilment:** When you are living a life that is designed according to your values, you are more likely to experience happiness and fulfillment.

- **Reduced Stress and Anxiety:** When you know what you are working towards, you are less likely to feel stressed or anxious about the future.

- **Improved Relationships:** When you are living a life that is true to yourself, you are better able to attract and maintain healthy relationships.

- **A More Fulfilling Career:** Design Your Life can help you identify your ideal career path and take steps to achieve your professional goals.

By taking time to demystify life and designing a holistic life of your aspirations, you can avoid the pitfalls that befell Robin, and many others. You can create a life that is filled with happiness, purpose, and success. "Design Your Life" is everyone's need. Exploring how to design your life is the core purpose of this book.

***

Chapter 2
Demystifying Life

The mystery of life is a deep question that has been pondered by philosophers and theologians for millennia. The idea that life's mysteries are roadblocks to success is interesting. So, perhaps a successful life isn't about completely demystifying everything, but about finding a balance. We can strive to understand ourselves and the world around us, while still cherishing the mysteries that spark our curiosity and keep life interesting. To understand life, do you have clear answer to following fundamental questions:

- What is life?
- What is the purpose of life?
- How to attain the purpose?

Unless people have clear understanding of above fundamental questions, they cannot demystify life and live according to their choice. People are living life either "by default" or "by design". Due to ignorance of fundamental questions, majority of people living life by default, which means their life is governed by external circumstances and they remain directionless and unhappy. If you wish to live a life according to your dreams and aspirations, you need to "design your life", but before that you must demystify life by finding answers to above questions.

Human beings are crown of creation, while it may always contain elements of mystery, it is also full of wonder, beauty, and potential. Incidentally, ancient scriptures - Vedas and

Upanishads demystify the life in most authentic and realistic manner.

Your beliefs and interpretations of life depends on your mindset, which may be either finite or infinite mindset. People with finite mindset, connect life with their physical existence only, linked with birth and death. They always live with fear of death or losing the possessions. On the other hand, people with infinite mindset believe life as infinite (*ananta*) journey, beyond time and space, they live life without fear and enjoy every moment of it. Enlightened seers describe life as infinite game, which is played not to win or lose, but to enjoy every moment of the game. Once you accept it as infinite game, there is no fear of losing or pride of winning, only playing to enjoy.

Life is an Infinite Game

"In the game of life, the only choice we get is whether we want to play with a finite mindset or an infinite mindset"

- There are two types of games we play in life; Finite, and Infinite Game. Finite games are like Chess, Football, etc. played with defined rules, an end point, and a winner.
- Infinite games are like business & politics, which has no fixed rules, and no end point, played to sustain the game itself, rather than to win.
- The notion of infinite mindset applies to life as well. There is no point to declare victory or quit.
- Life as *Anant*, is consciousness space beyond physical limitations, which can be experienced only by Spiritual awakening.

It is choice of the individual, what kind of mindset adopts, and how interprets various aspects of life. Infinite mindset facilitates the people to design and live a holistic and meaningful life, full of virtuous aspirations, challenges, and achievements. In this book effort has been made to demystify some complexities of life based on teachings of Upanishads, and figure out the parameters of life to facilitate "design your life" you wish to live.

2.1 What is life?

Life is an expression of consciousness, like the ocean in which waves rise and crash. Life is that wave, which identifies itself as a wave only, but in fact it is the ocean itself. In reality, human life is an infinite journey, similar to the wave of ocean, which in true sense water only. The wave after crashing becomes water, evaporates to become cloud, rains as water, freezes as snow on mountain peaks, melts to water, and flows in a river to merge with the same ocean where it came from, and this infinite cycle goes on and on forever.

Similar to journey of water, every person undergoes six modifications during life time; existence, birth, growth, old age, disease and death.

Journey of Life

During the moments of life, individuals perform physical and mental actions when come in contact of various beings, objects and situations of the world, and experience their share of happiness and sorrow. Life means activity, action is the signature of life, and final outcome of every action is an "experience". This transaction of actions and experiences is called life.

Human life is a continuous process, operating in a specific pattern with scientific reasoning to attain a set of goals. Life is manifestation of divinity, a continuous flow of existence, awareness and bliss. Life is a purposeful evolution from unreal to real, darkness to light, and from bondage to liberation. It is expressed in the world of objects in form of feelings, thoughts and actions through the human mind, intellect and body. Life is lived with actions and end result of every action is an experience. Life is a continuous series of experiences.

In this world of time and space, with every action we go on adding an experience. In this way along with time, life progresses in form of a continuous series of experiences.

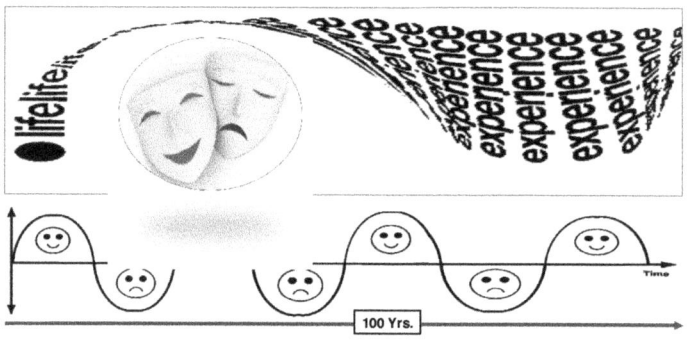

Life is a continuous series of Experiences

The quality of life of a person, depends upon the quality of experience gained from every action, when the actual result is according to desired outcome or expectation, the person experiences "happiness", but when the result of action is not according to desired outcome, the experience gained is "sorrow". To make life happier, we have to improve the quality of our experiences. The objective of life: seek maximum happiness for the maximum time.

2.2 Purpose of Life

Every object of this universe we can perceive or imagine has been created for a specific purpose. No object exists without purpose.

An object is defined as *anything that is perceived by senses, or something mental or physical toward which thought, feeling, or action is directed.*

Purpose of Life?

In this universe of time and space, except absolute consciousness (*Brahman*) everything (including human being) is considered as an object. Every object of this universe including being, product, process, event, system, organization or human being has an ultimate purpose that justifies its existence.

For example; the common perception about the ultimate purpose or *"bottom line"* of a business organization is to make profit. All business organizations of the world, whether they are in business of manufacturing, services, construction, computers, software, medicine, food, or anything, their final business performance is measured through the ultimate purpose - the *profit*. All activities and business processes of the organization are supposed to add value that ultimately contributes to the profit along with meeting the needs of its customers and other stakeholders. The clearer the purpose of the tasks being done by the people, the better the focus on their actions and the higher the probability of attaining the purpose.

Like every organization has an ultimate purpose for its existence, in the same way, every person including you and me also must have an ultimate purpose of life. The ultimate purpose inspires and propels us to perform actions to attain the purpose. The purpose of life is the central motivating goal - the reason we get up in the morning, prepare for work and perform our duties. Purpose guides life decisions, influences behavior shape's goal, offers a sense of direction, and creates meaning in life.

Do you know what is ultimate purpose of your life is? Why do you work? Can you clearly define and describe the ultimate purpose of your life?

Is the ultimate purpose of your life earning plenty of money, gain authority, build a successful career, recognition, status, or something else you are striving for?

Not everybody, but there are many people (maybe you also) in this world who have earned and possess plenty of wealth, authority, recognition, and all the objects of desire. After the accomplishment of all kinds of material prosperity, such people are still striving for something else too! What is that for which everyone including yourself is striving? What is the ultimate purpose of your life?

If you are not clear about the ultimate purpose of your life, do you think can you ever attain the ultimate goal for which you are striving? Is it possible to reach the final destination without knowing it?

Is it not surprising that without knowing what one truly wants, most people of this world go on working for some unknown things during their whole life? Finally, one day they leave this world and all they possessed during their lifetime, with unfulfilled desires.

According to Vedas, the ultimate purpose of everyone's life is "seek happiness". Whatever we are doing in life is ultimately to seek happiness only. But, due to ignorance, we set materialistic goals, and even after attaining them remain unhappy.

The Purpose of Life

- Life is perennial search for truth.
- The restless Swan - the human soul- on the journey infinite to find the truth.
- For thousands of years he is flying and flying with his wings outstretched and the will to reach the unscaled heights of heaven, higher and ever higher;
- The restless swan is on the journey infinite.
- He has all the blessings of mighty God, his piercing eyes perceive all the universe below, yet he knows no rest, no peace and keeps flying higher and ever higher;
- The restless swan is on the journey infinite.   - Rigveda

2.3 Inner Peace

Inner peace and happiness are the desired outcome of everyone's life. When a person attains inner peace, he or she becomes more creative, productive, and successful in all areas of personal and professional lives.

Inner peace is a state of mind when it is free from agitations (*chitta-vritti*), becomes quiet, gets connected with the Soul- the source of absolute "happiness" (*anand*). Inner peace and happiness can be understood by an example of a lake and moon.

Agitated Mind
(Disturbed & Unhappy)   **Agitation-free Mind**
                                            (Inner Peace & Happiness)

Imagine you are sitting near a beautiful lake in laps of Himalaya and enjoying the beauty of nature during a full-moon night. Surroundings of the lake are shining with cool soothing and milky moon light, silently sitting you are throwing small pebbles in the lake and watching the ripples of circular waves appearing on the water surface. Now you want to experience the coolness of the beautiful moon by bringing it in front of you, as a true reflection in the lake, but due to ripples on water surface, reflection of full moon is not appearing in its true shape in the lake and you can't feel the nearness of moon. To witness the moon near you, now you stopped throwing the pebbles and after sometime when all ripples disappeared, surface of the lake becomes still and reflective like a bright mirror. Full moon with its charming beauty appears in the lake and you get thrilled with a unique joy of happiness. The water of the lake is like mind (experiencer) and moon is like Soul (the source of happiness).

When water of lake is agitated and full of circular wave ripples on its surface, clear image of moon cannot be seen in the water, but when water is free from agitations and its surface becomes still like a mirror (peaceful), clear reflection of full moon appears in the lake. The same phenomena happens within us, when our mind is at peace (free from agitations), the reflection of Soul appears in the mind which is revealed as happiness.

Many ripple creating people, objects, events or situations will continue to come and go in your life, no matter whatever you do to control them. People face problems in physical, family, professional, and spiritual lives such as; serious disease, loss of dear ones, break ups, strained relationships, loss of job, financial loss in business, mental disturbances, etc. Life continues to move on. Such adverse conditions create mental agitations, under such situations only thing we need- inner peace.

The inner peace can be defined as *"a state of mind where calmness and satisfaction exist with all other unwanted factors being constant".*

True inner peace is independent of external conditions and circumstances, which can reveal lasting happiness. In the state of inner peace, unpleasant or adverse events cannot disturb your happiness. Spiritually realized saints or persons are unaffected by their physical problems or unpleasant situations, their mind remains at peace.

The practical spirituality develops capability to attain inner peace and happiness in simple and practical way. All it requires, your intense desire, commitment to learn and practice to move away from the chaos of current materialistic thinking and behavior. In state of inner peace, your Soul remains an observer, instead of allowing your mind to control everything happening around you. Mind gets detached from the worldly objects and conditions, therefore not affected by it. This practice will allow you to attain inner peace and happiness. This happens in the process of meditation.

2.4 Happiness

Whether you are an atheist or believer of God, materialist or spiritualist, scientist or philosopher, chief executive or a simple employee, irrespective of who you are, everyone is in constant search for happiness. During the journey of life, every person performs various actions, which are propelled by two commanding impulses;

- Longing for happiness, or
- Aversion from sorrow

In search of happiness, the person runs after all such objects and situations that he anticipates will make him happy, and tries to escape all such object and situations that he thinks may cause sorrow.

Happiness

The methods adopted by different individuals to gain happiness may be different depending upon their beliefs, knowledge, skills and resources, but ultimate goal remains the same. But do you really know what is happiness, where it comes from, and how is it accomplished? Let us understand the happiness...

Happiness according to Psychology

Psychologists view happiness as a multifaceted concept with two main components:

- **Subjective well-being:** This refers to your general sense of satisfaction with your life. It encompasses positive emotions like joy and contentment, but also includes a cognitive element - feeling your life is meaningful and worthwhile.

- **Positive emotions:** Experiencing more positive emotions than negative ones, are key part of happiness. This doesn't mean ignoring negative emotions, but rather focusing on cultivating positive feelings and having the resilience to bounce back from challenges.

People who are happy, experience the full range of human emotions, but they tend to have an underlying sense of optimism and well-being. Some people are naturally more predisposed to happiness than others. There are different paths to happiness, what makes one person happy might not be the same for another. It's important to find what works for you.

Happiness according to Positive Psychology

According to positive psychology, happiness can be described as an enduring state of mind consisting not only of feelings of joy, contentment, and other positive emotions, but also of a sense that one's life is meaningful and valued.

Positive Psychology Guru Martin Seligman describes that happiness has following three dimensions that can be cultivated. A fourth dimension was added by Sirgy and Wu (2009) as balanced life:

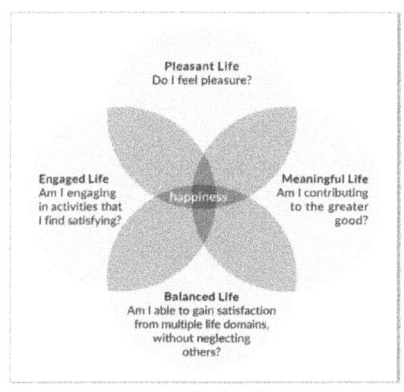

Happiness (Positive Psychology)

o **Pleasant life:** The regular experience of pleasantness.

o **Engaged life:** The frequent engagement in satisfying activities.

o **Meaningful life:** The experience of a

sense of connectedness to a greater whole.

- o **Balanced life:** Cultivating a sense of balance to satisfy broad spectrum of human needs from multiple domains.

Although each dimension is important, the happiest people tend to be those who pursue the full life - they infuse their life with pleasure, engagement, meaning and balance. Balance in life contributing to happiness because the amount of satisfaction derived from a single life domain is limited. One needs to be involved in multiple domains to satisfy the broad spectrum of human needs.

Happiness according to Vedanta

There are several interpretations of happiness, in different cultures and society. An authentic and profound definition of happiness given by Adi Shankaracharya in a scripture Tattva Bodh, as *"**Happiness** is the experience, gained when one is with oneself."* Thus, when one desires an object, performs actions to accomplish it, and after that desire is fulfilled, one feels happy. That momentary happiness is experienced because that makes one being with the one self. A happy person feels good, contented, relieved or satisfied after getting the desired thing.

Happiness is the fundamental and true nature of human being. The objects that appear to provide happiness for a moment are only the means, not the end. Objects by themselves do not possess capability to give happiness or sorrow, they are neutral.

Objects of desire are like wind, which clears the clouds that obstructs our vision of the sun. But the Sun is always present with its full brightness. Similarly, the *Self* - the source of infinite happiness, is always present within us like Sun, but we are not able to establish contact because of clouds of false knowledge, and mental agitations formed due to desires, which are obstructing it. When object of desire is obtained, a wind of satisfaction removes the cloud of mental agitations and establishes direct contact of Self with the mind experiencing the light of bliss.

Happiness is the final principle of value that motivates all perceptions, thoughts, and feelings, and thus it is ultimate result of whatever is perceived, thought about or felt through all experiences of the world.

Life is a continuous series of experiences. The nature of experience can be either positive or negative, expressed in form of happiness or sorrow. Happiness is a positive experience of life.

Happiness is the quest of all living beings - everyone seeks happiness, the materialist as well as spiritualist. Through our actions whether we seek good heath, plenty of wealth, pleasing relationships, success, recognition, authority or any other object of desire, what we are really seeking happiness only.

Happiness is the ultimate goal of life - the goal of all other means goals. We may be having so many means goals related to our physical, family, work and spiritual lives, but ultimate goal of all goals is to seek happiness only. Happiness is the peaceful state of mind. Let us analyze what is there in a person's mind, when he or she is happy?

Desire is sense of incompleteness, that compels us to perform actions to fulfill desire. As an individual, after obtaining a desired object when a person feels I am happy, it is a subjective feeling in the mind only, and it has nothing to do physically with the object. At that moment of happiness, mind is fully satisfied and does not desire that object any more, in other words, mind is in state of completeness. The agitation caused by desire has calmed down; mind has become serene and peaceful. When mind is peaceful, happiness is revealed. In other words, peace is happiness. Opposite to peace, when person's mind is agitated or disturbed, they become unhappy.

2.5 The Source of Happiness

Happiness is a unique experience, but where from it come? Psychologists and spiritualists explain the source of happiness in different ways.

Psychological View: There isn't one single source of happiness, according to psychology. Research suggests it's a combination of factors impacting your overall well-being. Here are some key contributors:

- **Strong Relationships:** Having close and supportive relationships with family, friends, and community is a major source of happiness. These connections provide a sense of belonging, love, and social support.

- **Meaning and Purpose:** Feeling like your life has a significant purpose is important. This purpose can come from your work, hobbies, personal goals, or even spiritual beliefs. It gives your life direction and motivates you.

- **Positive Outlook:** Optimists tend to be happier. This doesn't mean ignoring problems, but rather focusing on the positive and developing healthy coping mechanisms for challenges.

- **Security and Safety:** Feeling secure, both physically and emotionally, is crucial. This includes having your basic needs met (food, shelter, healthcare) and feeling safe from harm.

- **Personal Growth:** Continuously learning and growing as a person can be a great source of happiness. This can involve trying new things, developing your skills, and challenging yourself.

Remember, happiness is an ongoing process. By nurturing these different factors in your life, you can cultivate greater happiness and well-being.

Source of Happiness:
Spirit : the Soul or Inner Self

Nature of Spirit: सत चित आनंद
(Existence-Knowledge-Bliss)

True Source of Happiness

Spiritual View: According to *Vedas*, the true source of happiness (Ananda) is the Soul. It's true nature is "existence-knowledge-bliss". Unfortunately, due to materialistic mindset and ignorance of truth people are searching happiness in money, authority, wealth, objects, new companions, tourist places, cinema halls, clubs, even in alcohol and drugs, etc. Ultimately all the objects lead to sorrow only.

Except soul, no object has capability to provide happiness. To attain true and sustainable happiness we have to detach from the objective world and get attached to the inner Self.

2.6 Happiness Setpoint

The happiness set point is a concept in psychology that suggests we all have a natural baseline level of happiness that we tend to return to over time, regardless of life events.

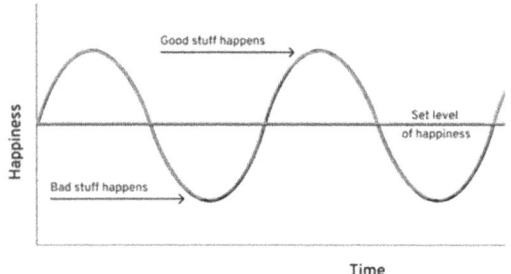

When we get a promotion, get divorced, have kids, or experience any other notable gain or loss in our life, we get an initial spike- either positive or negative-in our happiness level. However, as time goes on, the feeling of happiness or sadness caused by the change in conditions starts to dissipate until we're back around our set point of happiness.

It works like a thermostat for your mood. Events can push your happiness up or down, but eventually, you will move back to your set point.

Here's how it affects individuals:

- **Influence on Happiness Levels:** People with a high set point tend to be generally happy, while those with a low set point may experience more frequent dips in mood.

- **Genetics and Conditioning:** Genetics play a role in setting this baseline, but life experiences early on can also influence it.

- **Adaptation:** The set point theory is linked to the idea of hedonic adaptation, which is our tendency to adjust to both positive and negative situations. For instance, winning the lottery might give you a happiness boost, but over time, that excitement might lessen as your new circumstances become normal.

The happiness pie chart is a popular visualization tool used to represent the idea that different factors contribute to our overall happiness. It was developed by psychologists Sonja Lyubomirsky, Kennon M. Sheldon, and David Schkade based on their research. The happiness pie chart is typically divided into three slices based on genetics, circumstances, and intentionality in following proportion:

- **Genetics (50%):** This is the largest slice reflects the influence of our genes on our baseline happiness level.

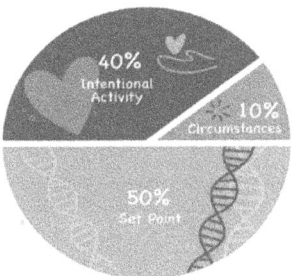

Happiness Pie Chart

- **Circumstances (10%):** This slice represents the impact of external factors like wealth, health, and relationships on happiness.

- **Intentional Activities (40%):** This is the largest slice, signifying the significant influence of our choices, behaviours, and activities on happiness.

While the happiness pie chart may not be a perfect representation of happiness, it serves as a helpful tool to understand that we have more control over our happiness than we might think. By focusing on activities and choices that cultivate positive emotions, fostering gratitude, building positive habits and resilience, we can work towards a happier and more fulfilling life.

2.8 How to attain Happiness

Happiness goes beyond just emotions. Psychology and spirituality both offer valuable insights on how to cultivate that deeper sense of connectedness with your inner self and achieve a more lasting happiness. Here's how they can work together:

Psychological Approach to Happiness

Practices like mindfulness can help you become more aware of your thoughts, feelings, and bodily sensations. This self-awareness allows you to identify negative patterns and choose more positive responses. Acceptance of difficult emotions without judgment and commit to living according to your values. This fosters inner peace and allows you to pursue what brings you meaning. Strengths-based approach focuses on identifying and utilizing your unique strengths. Using your talents builds confidence and satisfaction.

How to increase Happiness: Sonja Lyubomirsky, a leading researcher in happiness, identified following activities that can increase happiness;

1. **Expressing Gratitude:** Taking time to appreciate the good things in your life, both big and small, can boost happiness. You can do this by keeping a gratitude journal, writing thank-you notes, or simply taking a moment each day to reflect on the things you're grateful for.
2. **Cultivating Optimism:** Having a positive outlook on life can make a big difference in your happiness. There are a number of things you can do to cultivate optimism, such as focusing on the good things in life, challenging negative thoughts, and setting realistic goals.

3. **Avoiding Overthinking & Social Comparison:** Overthinking, is when you repetitively dwell on the same thought or situation over and over to the point that it disrupts your life. Overthinking usually falls into two categories: ruminating about the past and worrying about the future. To avoid overthinking change the channel in your brain by changing your activity. Doing something different will put an end to the barrage of negative thoughts.

   The social comparison process involves people coming to know themselves by evaluating their own attitudes, abilities, and traits in comparison with others. This creates superiority or inferiority complex, both reduce happiness.

4. **Practicing Acts of Kindness:** Helping others is a great way to boost your happiness. There are many ways to be kind, such as volunteering your time, donating to charity, or simply doing something nice for a friend or family member

5. **Nurturing Social Relationships:** Strong social relationships are essential for happiness. Make time for the people who are important to you, and invest in building new relationships.

6. **Developing Strategies for Coping:** Coping is what people do to alleviate the hurt, stress, or suffering caused by negative event or situation.

7. **Learning to Forgive:** Holding on to anger and resentment can only hurt you in the long run. Forgiveness is a gift you give yourself, not to the other person. There are many ways to forgive someone, and what works for one person may not work for another.

The important thing is to find a way to let go of the negative feelings and move on.

8. **Increasing Flow Experiences:** Flow is a state of complete absorption in an activity, where time seems to fly by and you're completely focused on the task at hand. Flow experiences can be very enjoyable and can lead to a sense of accomplishment. You can increase your flow experiences by finding activities that challenge you but are also within your skill level.

9. **Savouring Life's Joys:** Take the time to savour the good things in life, both big and small. This could involve spending time in nature, listening to your favourite music, or spending time with loved ones.

10. **Committing to Your Goals:** Setting and working towards goals can give your life a sense of direction and purpose. When you achieve a goal, it can give you a great sense of satisfaction.

11. **Practicing Religion & Spirituality:** One major benefit from practicing religion is the benefit of social net-working. Social connections are a genuine source of happiness. Those who attend religious services feel a strong sense of identity. People with an intense sense of spirituality learn to relish in the moment. Make a point to pray for a period of time each day, a prayer of gratitude is especially helpful.

12. **Taking Care of Your Body:** This includes eating a healthy diet, getting regular exercise, and getting enough sleep. When you take care of your body, you feel better physically and mentally.

By incorporating some of these activities into your life, you can increase your happiness and well-being.

Spiritual Approach to Happiness

Vedanta philosophy has a unique perspective on happiness that goes beyond fleeting pleasures. The greatest teacher of the universe - Lord Krishna advised Arjun "Chose to be Happy".

Happiness is a Choice

- According to Bhagavad Gita; happiness is not just a fleeting emotion or a result of external factors, but **a state of being that arises from spiritual connection**, inner peace, contentment, and living a life aligned with one's true purpose.
- Happiness is a **choice** that can be cultivated through our thoughts, actions, and attitudes. Living a happy and fulfilling life to achieve greater harmony and balance within ourselves and the world around us.

Connecting to something larger than yourself, whether it's a cause, spiritual practice, or a deep connection to nature, can provide a sense of direction and purpose. Here's how Vedanta approaches enhancing happiness:

- **True Self vs. Ego:** Vedanta distinguishes between the Atman (true Self) and the ego. The ego, driven by desires and attachments, is the source of unhappiness. Happiness comes from realizing your true Self, which is pure consciousness and bliss (Ananda) itself.

- **Impermanence and Detachment:** The world is seen as Maya (illusion), ever-changing and ultimately unreal. Chasing worldly pleasures for happiness is like chasing a mirage. Vedanta teaches detachment from external objects and desires, leading to a more stable form of happiness.

- **Understanding Happiness:** Vedanta identifies two types of happiness:
  - **Sukha (Pleasure):** This is fleeting pleasure derived from external things, money, relationships, etc. It's temporary and leads to suffering when it ends.
  - **Ananda (Bliss):** This is the inherent blissful nature of the true Self. It's permanent, independent of external circumstances, and the ultimate source of happiness.
- **Path to Self-Realization:** Vedanta offers various paths to realize your true Self and experience Ananda. These include:
  - **Jnana Yoga (Path of Knowledge):** Studying scriptures and teachings to understand the nature of reality.
  - **Bhakti Yoga (Path of Devotion):** Developing love and devotion for a higher power.
  - **Karma Yoga (Path of Action):** Performing actions selflessly, without attachment to the fruits of those actions.

By following these approaches, you can move beyond fleeting pleasures and experience lasting happiness rooted in your true nature. Practice of yoga and meditation, and expressing appreciation can shift your focus to the positive aspects of life.

Practicing gratitude is a path to happiness. Developing compassion for yourself and others fosters a sense of connection and reduces negativity. Remember, the key is finding what works for you. Experiment with different approaches and see how psychology and spirituality can guide you towards a more connected and joyful existence.

***

Chapter 3
The Sailboat Metaphor

A historical and inspiring "sailboat" journey Navika Sagar Parikrama successfully circumnavigated the globe by a six member women officers of Indian Navy during 2017-18, led by Lieutenant Commander Vartika Joshi. Their sailboat INSV **Tarini** was a specifically designed for long voyages. While modern and well-equipped, it still relied on the power of the wind and the skill of the crew to navigate the vast oceans. The unique sailboat voyage broke barriers and showed the world the capabilities of Indian women at sea. The voyage lasted 254 days, with four port calls in Australia, New Zealand, Falkland Islands, South Africa, and a technical halt at Port Louis, Mauritius, crossing the equator twice and passing through three oceans. The voyage on INSV Tarini was fraught with danger, many times the crew was caught up in gale and faced waves as high as nine-storey building with speed up to 120 kmph. The crew also suffered from extreme weather conditions, starting with 45 degrees Celsius

Sailboat TARINI

temperature in India, 12 degrees in Australia, 0 degree in New Zealand and sub-zero in Pacific Ocean. The brave crew of INSV Tarini, after completing their epic journey reached Goa on 21 May 2018 after completing 21980 nautical miles journey. Their success is a testament to their seamanship and resilience. This is an ideal analogy to manage our life journey using sailboat metaphor.

In the journey of life, we can learn valuable lessons from the grace and resilience of Tarini sailboat crew, successfully navigated the vast sea. Just as Tarini sailboat relied on the wind; to propel it forward, we too must harness the power of our inner resources and external support systems to navigate the ebbs and flows of our lives. The destination of life, only as good as the journey. A great journey does not only take you from one place to another, it allows you to explore the world and embrace the experiences of its beauty and joy at every moment of life.

The sailboat journey used as metaphor by positive psychologists to design and live a life that involves understanding various aspects of the navigating sailboat in the sea, and how they relate to human life.

Imagine your life as a journey on a sailboat. The sturdy hull (boat) represents your core foundation, the one that keeps you afloat. The wind, ever-changing, reflects the unexpected challenges and opportunities that life throws your way. To harness this wind and reach your destination, you'll need a billowing sail, symbolizing your goals and aspirations. As you navigate the vast waters, which represent the ever-shifting world around you, this metaphor will guide you in making adjustments, finding balance, and ultimately, charting your own course towards a fulfilling life.

Whether you are an experienced sailor or know nothing, you will find a comprehensive approach that will inspire you to discover new ways of looking at life through the sailboat metaphor.

The Sailboat Metaphor is a psychological tool originally designed by Hugo Alberts, a psychologist, researcher, entrepreneur, and professor of psychology at the University of Maastricht, Netherlands. The concept presented in this book has been modified by the author as psycho-spiritual approach to give holistic perspective to sailboat metaphor.

This metaphor beautifully illustrates how human beings function by comparing human life to a sailboat journey. It's a very simple, yet multi-faceted perspective on the self, and understanding this metaphor can help people to understand themselves in a better way. In this book, the sailboat metaphor integrates and synergizes practical spirituality concepts of the Holy *Vedas*, with positive psychology and design thinking, in a rational and practical way.

The sailboat metaphor has eleven distinct elements, which are used to design, sail, monitor, and navigate the sailboat journey in the right direction to reach the desired destination. The human life is metaphorically similar to the sailboat journey, which is used to translate the life philosophy into practically implementable steps. The sailboat metaphor is holistically applied to "Design Your Life" initiative taken by progressive people to design and live the life they aspire to.

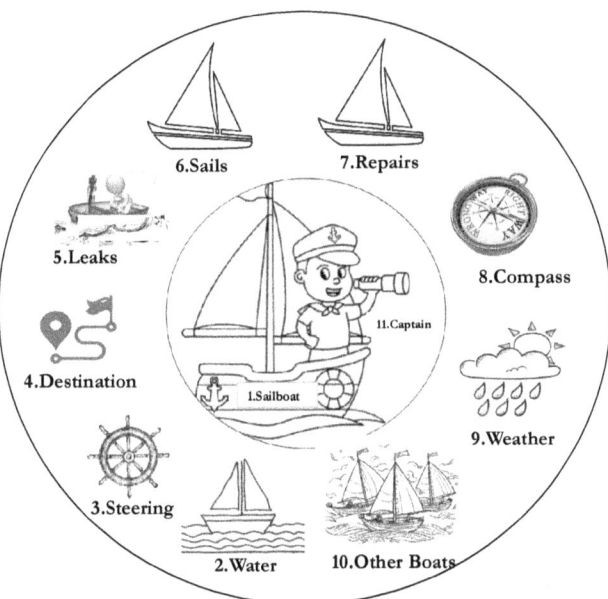

Elements of Sailboat Metaphor

As shown in the figure, there are eleven elements in the sailboat metaphor. A brief description is presented here:

Sailboat Metaphor		
#	*Elements*	*Role in Sailboat*	*How it works in Life*
1	Sailboat	Sailboat- the ship performing journey	It is you- your personality, through which you are going to perform your life journey.
2	Water	The pathway of the sailboat	Your four domains of life; physical, family, work, and spiritual- pathways of your life.
3	Steering	Sets & controls the direction of the sailboat	Your personal values, life & work views set and control the direction of your life.
4	Destination	Objectives and Goals of Journey.	Objectives and goals of your life.

5	**Leaks**	Holes and defects of sailboat causing leaks	Personal weaknesses and negative behaviours that hinder your progress.
6	**Sails**	Strengths and capabilities of sails	Personal strengths - your knowledge, skills, and positive attitude that supports your progress.
7	**Repairs**	Solving problems of sailboats	Solving problems of life using problem-solving techniques.
8	**Compass**	Feedback of direction of the journey	An internal feedback mechanism - experiences, emotions, and intuitions about your journey
9	**Weather**	Stormy, turbulent, and uncontrollable weather on the sea	Unpleasant and uncontrollable events, and circumstances encountered in life
10	**Other Boats**	Other boats sailing around you	Other people around you who influence your life journey.
11	**Captain**	Commander of the Sailboat	You, as commander of your life.

Each element is not only crucial to the functioning of the sailboat, but is also a symbol of an important aspect of living a fulfilling life. In this book, various elements are interpreted by combining the basic concepts of positive psychology with ancient *Vedantic* wisdom of spirituality.

In the end, the sailboat is not just a metaphor—it is a mirror reflecting the essence of your being, the journey of your soul. So, hoist your sails high, dear Captain, and let the winds of destiny carry you forth. Your journey of life is not about reaching a destination only, but embracing the journey itself with all its twists and turns, its joys and sorrows, its triumphs and tribulations.

3.1 Sailboat

The "sailboat" represents the "individual" who performs the life journey. Just as a sailboat is a vessel performing its journey across the water of vast ocean, an individual performs his/her life journey in the vast physical world.

Like a sailboat exploring uncharted sea waters, individuals embark on a journey of self-discovery, growth, and personal development, navigating through the unknown environment to reach their destinations.

Just as sailors use navigational instruments to plot their course, individuals rely on their experiences (emotions, feelings, and intuition) to guide their decisions and actions, steering toward their goals and aspirations. Like a sailboat, that moves forward with the wind's energy, individuals progress on their life journey by embracing new experiences, overcoming obstacles, and expanding their horizons. Each journey taken by the sailboat of life offers opportunities for growth, learning, self-discovery, resilience-building, and personal evolution. The sailboat also reflects the individual's identity, values, and aspirations. Just as each sailboat is unique in its design and features, every individual brings their unique strengths, passions, and dreams to their life journey. The choices made in steering the sailboat reflect the individual's values, priorities, and vision for their life.

Overall, the sailboat represents you and your holistic personality through which you are going to navigate through life's experiences, challenges, and opportunities. By taking up the role, of the captain of your sailboat, you can embark on a life journey toward your desired destinations using the "Design Your Life" framework.

3.2 Water

In the sailboat metaphor, "water" represents the "pathway" on which the sailboat moves toward its destination. Similarly, in human life, water represents the world of the physical environment, circumstances, and challenges that individuals encounter as they navigate through life. A sailboat can't move without water; you cannot function without the environment that you live in and interact with. This environment is your direct "physical reality", characterized by many factors including your health, family, job, possessions, inner-self and geographical location. In short, it is your direct physical reality. Water symbolizes the external environment and circumstances in which individuals find themselves. As per the Vedic concepts, human beings are born with four natural constituents of personality- body, mind, intellect, and spirit. Accordingly, they function in an environment with four core domains of life; physical life, family life, work life, and spiritual life. These four core domains become the pathways of life on which individual has to sail their life that shapes their actions and experiences.

Like the unpredictable nature of the sea, life's waters can be dynamic and ever-changing, presenting individuals with both challenges and opportunities as they navigate their journey.

The challenges, obstacles, and problems that individuals encounter along their path may include failures, disappointments, and hardships that provide opportunities for growth, learning, transformation, resilience, and wisdom through problem-solving.

Overall, water in the sailboat metaphor represents the dynamic and ever-changing nature of life, with its challenges, opportunities, uncertainties, and interconnectedness. By navigating life's waters with courage, resilience, and mindfulness, you can embark on life's journey toward your desired destination, embracing the journey with grace and determination.

3.3 Steering

In the sailboat metaphor, steering is an important element to set and control the direction of the sailboat. Similarly, "steering" represents your "personal values", which are important to select the way you live and work. The purpose of steering in a sailboat is to steer the boat in the desired direction. Similarly, your values serve as the steering wheel of your life and help you steer in the desired direction. Personal values are a set of guiding principles and beliefs that help you differentiate between "good" (right direction) and "bad" (wrong direction).

Values are extensions of your personality, define and inform priorities, guide you to take actions, decisions, and choices, help individuals to shape their character, and set the goals and destination of life. Every person is knowingly or unknowingly driven by certain values which may lead to progress or downfall resulting in happiness or sorrow.

Good values are factually based and constructive, and you can control them. You also develop them internally. Some of the good values that take you in the right direction are; gratitude, integrity, self-discipline, humility, compassion, empathy, service, perseverance, love, truth, patriotism, respect, etc.

Bad values are non-factual, non-constructive, and out of your control, are harmful to yourself and others, it takes you in the wrong direction in life. Examples of bad values include; greed, ego, lust for money, dishonesty, materialism, hatred, fear, etc.

Everyone prioritizes their core values differently based on their experiences of happiness, meaning, and fulfilment that decide the direction of their life.

To know whether the direction of your life is right or wrong, another element of the sailboat- "compass" is used. Based on the information from the compass, the steering wheel is used for course correction.

When your behaviour aligns with your values, you are in a state of happiness and well-being. But when you are disconnected from your values - your behaviour and values don't align, you feel a sense of discontent, like something is not right, which can be the cause of unhappiness.

3.4 Destination

In the sailboat metaphor "destination" represents the ultimate "objectives and goals" that individuals aim to achieve in their physical, family, work, and spiritual domains

of lives. Just as a sailor navigates the ship toward a specific destination, individuals set sailboats toward their life goals, guided by their values, life views, and work views.

Without a destination or waypoints, the sailboat is likely to be lost in the sea exposed to all sorts of danger, and at the risk of damage and sinking in the sea. So, if you don't have clear goals, you don't know your destination, which means you are not going to reach anywhere, no matter how hard you work or how competent you are.

Destination is the desired outcome that individuals strive to reach. This destination may evolve as individuals grow, learn, and reassess their priorities at different stages of life. It serves as a signal, guiding individuals toward a future state of fulfilment, success, wellness, and happiness. While the destination may seem distant or elusive, it provides a sense of purpose and direction, inspiring individuals to persevere through challenges and obstacles encountered along the way.

Goals in the sailboat metaphor are similar to the destinations or waypoints that sailors aim to reach during their journey. These goals can be short-term or long-term, specific or general, and may encompass various aspects of life, including; health, lifestyle, relationships, play, career, personal development, wealth creation, spiritual, and holistic well-being. Setting specific, measurable, achievable, realistic, and time-bound goals provide individuals with direction and purpose, helping them stay value-focused and motivated as they navigate their life journey. In a nutshell, the destination and goals in the sailboat metaphor symbolize the journey of personal growth, achievement, and fulfilment in the core domains of life.

3.5 Leaks

Leaks in the Sailboat

The leaks in the sailboat are something that can retard the progress of the journey or make the boat sink, if it is not repaired in time. The "leaks" represent "personal weaknesses" or challenges that reduce individual's well-being and happiness in life. A weakness is anything that hinders proper functioning and retards growth, prevents living personal values and achieving goals, disturbs inner peace, and makes us unhappy.

The leaks in a sailboat allow water to seep in and potentially slow down or sink the vessel. Actions to fetch out the leaking water, or plug the leak consume energy, effort, and time, retards progress. The leaks occur due to some holes in the hull or defects in the main body of the boat, inadequate strength and capability of a sailboat, and inefficient navigation of the sailboat.

Similarly leaks in your life appear as personal weaknesses in your physical, psychological, intellectual, and spiritual behaviours. Due to leaks (personal weaknesses), people make wrong decisions, poor actions, mistakes, and unpleasant behaviour that hamper growth and success in life. These leaks drain valuable energy, time, effort, and resources for rectification. Identifying and addressing these metaphorical leaks is essential for maintaining progress and resilience on life's journey.

3.6 Sails

In the sailboat metaphor, the function of sails is to harness the power of the wind and convert it into the forward motion of the sailboat. Just like a sailboat needs both a sturdy hull and powerful "sails" to propel forward and help reach its full potential, similarly to for a successful journey your life needs "personal strengths" and capabilities to propel your life forward to achieve personal growth and desired goals.

In the life journey, personal growth and success are achieved by enhancing the strengths of your personality. Every individual is born with four natural resources; body, mind, intellect, and spirit as integral constituents of personality. These four resources provide power to propel the individual to perform a life journey in the world, similar to sails that propel the sailboat to move toward its destination. By enhancing the personal strengths of the physical, psychological, intellectual, and spiritual constituents of personality and harnessing them to navigate through life with greater resilience, efficiency, and effectiveness. These personal strength factors are positive traits reflected in thoughts, feelings, actions and behaviours.

To attain success and happiness in life, positive psychology emphasizes the continuous enhancement of personal strengths of personality, rather than focusing solely on weaknesses and plugging the leaks.

3.7 Repairs

During sailing, a sailboat faces some minor or major breakdowns or wear and tear due to various adverse circumstances, to continue a smooth journey it is essential to repair and maintain the sailboat to keep it fit to continue the journey. Similarly in life, we encounter many kinds of problems, which adversely affect progress and quality of life. It becomes essential to solve such problems to resume our life journey.

In the sailboat metaphor, "repair" represents "problem-solving" or addressing issues that arise in your life, relationships, or endeavours. Repair involves identifying and defining the problems, ideating solutions, selecting the best solution, developing prototype, testing, and implementing solutions to restore normal conditions. Design thinking framework is one of the most effective techniques to solve problems.

In real life, repair can manifest in various forms depending on the context. It might involve repairing damaged relationships through communication, forgiveness, and compromise. In professional settings, it could mean rectifying mistakes, resolving conflicts, or improving processes to enhance efficiency and productivity. Personal development also often involves repairing aspects of ourselves that may be holding us back, whether it's overcoming limiting beliefs, healing from past traumas, or cultivating healthier habits. Ultimately, repair is about acknowledging and addressing problems proactively to restore balance, resilience, and progress.

3.8 Compass

In the sailboat metaphor, the compass works as a feedback system and allows sailors to maintain a desired course by referencing a specific direction (e.g., north, south, etc.). In addition to giving direction feedback, a compass helps in course correction. If the sailboat strays off course due to wind or currents, the compass helps identify the deviation and allows for adjustments to bring the sailboat back on track.

The "compass" represents the "inner guidance system" that individuals rely on to navigate the journey of life with clarity, purpose, and integrity. By staying true to their values, and life views, individuals can chart a path towards their desired destination (goals) with confidence and determination. The compass of your life can give you feedback, on whether you are heading in the right direction. It works as an emotional thermometer, if you are on the right path, compass will reflect your well-being. Conversely, if you feel any discomfort, it warns you to retrospect and take course correction.

In real-life situations, every facet of your life is under the control of the mind. Your mind operates like a compass used by the captain of the sailboat, which provides insight into the direction and course of life's journey relative to goals, aspirations, and destinations. Your ultimate life objective (happiness) and personal values serve as the true north, and your mind acts as the needle or indicator of the compass.

Overall, the compass serves as a powerful symbol for navigating both the open seas and the vast ocean of life. By having a sense of direction and making adjustments as needed, you can ensure a smooth and purposeful journey.

3.9 Weather

In the sailboat metaphor, "weather" represents the "external circumstances" or conditions that the sailor encounters during the sea journey. Just as weather conditions can change rapidly at sea, life's circumstances can vary unpredictably, presenting individuals with challenges, adversities, and obstacles along their life journey. These challenges may come in various forms such as; the loss of a loved one, getting stuck in traffic, divorce, breakup, losing the job, accidents, setbacks, failures, loss in business, conflicts, disappointments, etc.

Navigating through such uncertain weather conditions require individuals to stay flexible, open-minded, and adaptive, adjusting their course as needed to navigate through changing winds and currents.

A sailboat has to be prepared to deal with rough weather or storms. Having strong sails is the most important way to prepare for bad weather conditions because if the sails are unable to withstand wear, pressure, or damage, the strong winds of the storm will tear the sails and the sailboat will be at the risk of capsizing and sinking.

Despite its challenges, weather also presents opportunities for growth, learning, and transformation. Positive life events or experiences help you grow and flourish and allow you to make the most of your strengths. The negative life events or experiences can have a more serious and adverse impact on your well-being depending on how you deal with them. The ability to deal with these adverse circumstances effectively can build resilience and help people to stay on the right track, despite any challenges that accompany the circumstances.

Overall, the weather in the sailboat metaphor represents the external circumstances and internal challenges that individuals encounter as they navigate their journey through life. By embracing life's weather with courage, resilience, mindfulness, and spiritual awareness individuals can navigate through storms and sunshine alike, charting a course toward their desired destination with grace and determination.

3.10 Other Boats

In the sea journey sailboat does not move alone, it is surrounded by several "other boats" also, which may influence the sailboat's journey. They are also important for the smooth functioning of a sailboat because a sailboat has to ensure that it's not getting in the path of other boats, or they are not crossing its path or sailing too close together. Sometimes, collisions may happen between boats when sailing too close together.

Positive, Neutral, & Negative People

Similarly in your life journey, you are not alone, but surrounded by many "other persons". The people that you are surrounded with, may influence you in many ways, which can be positive, negative, or neutral. Think of all the people around you such as your spouse, parents, siblings, children, teachers, friends, boss, colleagues, etc. who have been a great influence, positive or negative, on you, your life, your choices, and your decisions. The people (other boats) in life can be broadly classified into three categories;

- **Positive people**- the people who have a positive influence on you. They believe in you and teach you to believe in yourself. They support you, motivate you, encourage you, and push you to grow yourself because they want you to be happy and successful. They are your life support system and come to your rescue, like a lifeboat that rescues people from a sinking ship. These are the people who matter the most to you in your life.
- **Negative people**- the people who don't believe in you and make you doubt yourself and question your choices and decisions. They are toxic; they actively oppose you, undermine you, demotivate and discourage you, and try to bring out the worst in you, because they are envious of you and want you to fail

and be unhappy. These are the people you need to keep a distance from them
- **Neutral people**- who are indifferent to your life, not going to influence you in any way.

Overall, other boats in the sailboat metaphor represent the external influences, interactions, and relationships that individuals encounter as they navigate their journey through life. By recognizing and navigating these external factors with awareness, resilience, and collaboration, individuals can chart a course toward their desired destination with greater clarity, purpose, and fulfilment.

3.11 Captain

The captain of the sailboat plays the main role in deciding the course, direction and destination of journey, and solving the problems encountered during the journey, till attains its goals.

Similarly, as Captain of your life journey, you take control of your destiny, recognizing that you have the power to influence the direction of your life through your choice, actions, and mindset. It involves being proactive rather than reactive and taking ownership of your decisions and their consequences.

By embracing your role as the architect of your destiny, you empower yourself to "design your life" you aspire to. This involves setting clear goals, making strategic plans, and taking decisive action to move towards your destination and life goals.

Everything cannot go exactly as per your plan, you need to adapt and learn from setbacks, persevere through challenges, and continuously adjust your course as needed.

Ultimately, by taking charge of your destiny, you shape your narrative and carve out a fulfilling and purposeful life aligned with your values, passions, and aspirations.

***

Chapter 4
Life You Wish to Live

Life you wish to live isn't about some fantasy future. Life of your choice is not something predetermined, it's up to you to design. It's about identifying the values and passions that truly resonate with you, the things that make you feel fulfilled. Imagine your life as a masterpiece waiting to be crafted as you wish to live. Every experience, every relationship, every achievement – a brushstroke on your personal canvas. Why is this important? Because the reality is, the experiences that shape you, that bring you joy and purpose, largely depend on the choices you make today. By designing your life, you're not just picking a path, you're actively curating a collection of experiences that will define you. Think about it, would you leave the design of your dream house to random chance? Of course not! The same goes for your life. By investing time and intention into its design, you're setting yourself up for a life of fulfilment and satisfaction.

Design Your Life is not about blind chance; it's about taking control and creating a life rich with the things that matters most to you. This book is here to guide you through that process. By getting clear on what your ideal life looks like, you can make choices that align with your deepest desires, not external circumstances. This will be the foundation for a life that feels intentional and brings you genuine happiness. It's your life, and you get to design it.

So, before you dive into the twelve steps of design your life, take a moment to consider the incredible power you hold. You are the architect of your own experience. Let's design something truly remarkable!

4.1 A Well-Designed Life

A well-designed life, considering the four natural personality constituents (physical, emotional, intellectual, and spiritual), fosters growth and balance in each area. Imagine it like a well-maintained garden, where each section flourishes and contributes to the overall beauty and health of the whole.

Here's how a well-designed life can take care of each constituent:

- **Physical:** Prioritizes healthy habits like exercise, good nutrition, and quality sleep. It allows for activities you enjoy and that keep your body strong and vibrant.

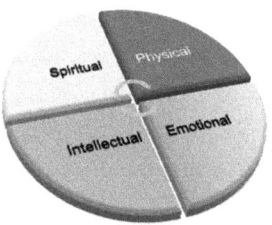

Four domains of Holistic Life

- **Emotional:** Cultivates healthy relationships, fosters self-compassion, and practices emotional regulation techniques. It allows you to experience a full range of emotions in a healthy way.

- **Intellectual:** Engages your curiosity through learning new things, exploring different ideas, and challenging yourself mentally. It allows you to keep your mind sharp and expand your knowledge.

- **Spiritual:** Connects you to something larger than yourself. You strive for inner peace and mindfulness, finding ways to manage stress and cultivate a sense of contentment, and quietude. This could be through spiritual learning and practices, nature, or simply a sense of purpose. It provides meaning and direction in life.

Balancing Act: A well-designed life doesn't require equal focus on each area all the time. Life has seasons, and your needs will shift. The key is to be intentional about nurturing each aspect and ensuring none is consistently neglected.

Signs of a Well-Designed Life: Here are some indicators that your life design is working:

- You feel energized and have a sense of well-being.
- You have strong, supportive relationships.
- You feel challenged and fulfilled by your work or pursuits.
- You experience a sense of purpose and meaning in life.

Continuous Process: Remember, "design your life" is not a onetime activity, it is a continuous process. As you grow and learn, your needs and priorities may change. Regularly revisit your design, make adjustments, and keep nurturing all aspects of your being. By doing this, you'll cultivate a life that is flourishing, balanced, and truly your own.

4.2 The GPS of your Life

Beliefs, Values, and Rules of Life: According to psychology, all decisions and actions of your life are governed by three key elements; beliefs, values, and rules. These are global positioning system of your life.

Imagine you're on a road trip to your favorite vacation place, but instead of a map, you have three key tools: a compass (your Values), a set of guiding principles (your Rules), and a belief system about the journey itself (your Beliefs). A famous motivator and author Tony Robbins, explains in his book *Awakening the Giant Within*, following three elements are crucial for designing your life. Here's how they work in your life:

- **Beliefs:** These are your fundamental convictions about yourself, the world, and how things work. Beliefs can be limiting or empowering. They answer questions like "Am I capable?" or "Is the world a fair place?". Beliefs shape your perception of reality and your potential.

    To reveal your belief- *Ask yourself:*

    o What are my core beliefs about myself (e.g., confident, worthy)?

    o What are my beliefs about the world (e.g., abundant, fair)?

    o Are these beliefs empowering or limiting?

- **Values:** These are the principles that guide your decisions and what you hold dear. They represent what's truly important to you, like honesty, kindness, or adventure. Values evolve over time. What matters most to you: is it family, adventure, creativity, or something else entirely? Your values are your core principles, your non-negotiables in life. They act as your compass, guiding your direction of life and decisions towards what truly fulfils you.

To discover your Value - *Reflect on:*

- What truly matters to me in life (e.g., happiness, growth, connection)?
- What principles do I want to guide my decisions?
- How would I describe my ideal life based on these values?

- **Rules of Life:** These are the specific guidelines you set for yourself based on your values and beliefs. They are the "how-to" that translate your beliefs and values into action. How will you live by your values? For example, if "honesty" is a value, your rule might be "always be truthful, even when it's difficult." Rules need to be adaptable. Life throws curveballs, so you should be flexible, while staying true to your core principles

Reform your rules- *Turn your values into actionable rules:*

- How can I live each day in alignment with my values (e.g., spend quality time with loved ones, pursue a learning opportunity)?
- Create specific rules that translate your values into daily habits.

By diving deep into your Beliefs, Values, and Rules, you gain clarity on the foundation you are building your life on. This self-awareness empowers you to make conscious choices that propel you towards a life that feels authentic and fulfilling. Remember, your life's design is in your hands – use these blueprints to craft a masterpiece!

4.3 Designer Mindset

Design your life is a challenging task, it requires a unique mindset with purity of intention, clarity of knowledge, bias for action, and faith & self-confidence. To attain success in any endeavour of life, as per spiritual philosophy, we need four kinds of natural power;

- *Iccha Shakti*: Will power,
- *Gyan Shakti*: Knowledge power,
- *Kriya Shakti:* Action power, and
- *Aatm Shakti:* Spiritual power

Design Your Life uses principles of positive psychology, practical spirituality, and follows five phases of design thinking; empathize, define, ideate, prototype and test. To integrate natural powers with design thinking concepts, Design Your Life (DYL) requires a unique mindset with; Strong Desire, Curiosity to learn, Bias for action, and Faith & Self-confidence:

- **Strong Desire:** In DYL, the first step is understanding yourself. This aligns with the concept of strong desire (Iccha Shakti) but with a twist. Instead of just focusing on **what** you want, DYL emphasizes **why** you want it. Use empathy to connect with your inner self to understand your desires deeply. What truly excites you? What kind of life would bring you fulfilment? This introspection will help you craft a strong life view (your dream) that fuels your desire and motivates you throughout the design process.

- **Curiosity to Learn:** Curiosity is the engine of knowledge (Gyan Shakti). Here, curiosity is about understanding yourself, the world around you, and the possibilities that exist. Gyan Shakti, the knowledge power, translates your desire to experimentation. Build prototype versions of your ideas to test them in the real world and gain valuable insights. Your curiosity encourages you to see challenges as opportunities to learn and iterate. Instead of fixating on one path, be curious about possibilities. Research different careers, explore hobbies, and talk to people with diverse experiences. Be open to adapting your goals and approaches based on new information.

- **Bias for Action:** "Kriya Shakti" (action power) propels your "Bias for Action." Life design emphasizes taking action and learning from the results. Don't get stuck in the planning phase. Once you have a basic idea, take action and see how it works. Experiment! Try new things, take small courses, or shadow someone in your desired field. DYL emphasizes continuous iteration and feedback. Test your prototypes, gather feedback, and refine your approach based on what you learn. After testing and validation of your prototype, implement the design in your life.
- **Faith & Self-Confidence:** "Aatm Shakti" or spiritual energy comes from the faith in divine power, provides a sense of inner strength and purpose, that develops self-confidence. It assures you that you're not alone and that a greater power is supporting you. Faith can act as a guiding light, providing direction and meaning in life. This clarity allows you to make decisions with conviction and navigate challenges with a sense of purpose. Spiritual faith can offer comfort and security. It can help you confront fears, and allows you to take risks and step outside your comfort zone with greater confidence.

By incorporating these mindsets, you can design a life that aligns with your deepest desires, leverages your curiosity, and fuels your drive to take action.

***

Chapter 5
Design Your Life

By now, you are well acquainted with all elements of sailboat metaphor, which are symbolically representing various aspects of your life. To live a fulfilling and holistic life all elements of sailboat must be addressed. Ask yourself;

- Do you ever feel like you are drifting through life without a clear direction?
- Do you wonder what your purpose is, and how to achieve your goals?

Design your life activities can help you navigate these uncertainties. Through a series of powerful exercises, you will gain clarity on:

- Who you are?
- Where are you now on your life path?
- What is direction and destination of your life?
- What are your weaknesses and strengths?
- What are challenges of your life? and
- How to navigate life in the right direction, while facing the rough weathers and maintaining harmony with people around you?

Before moving further, take time to reflect on the above question and find your answers based on your present beliefs. There may be some true or false beliefs, you may be aware on unaware but driving your present life. To design a life of your aspirations, life design begins with changing your beliefs.

5.1 Life Design - Changing Your Beliefs

Understanding Your Belief System: Every life unfolds like a story, shaped by the invisible threads of our beliefs. These beliefs, a unique tapestry woven from experience, shape our perception, guide our choices, and ultimately, design our reality.

But what exactly is a belief? A belief is a conviction we hold about ourselves, the world, or how things work. These convictions can be formed consciously, through experience or education. However, many beliefs are established subconsciously, during our formative years, absorbing them from family, culture, or society.

The key to remember is that beliefs, whether true or false, hold power. They act as a filter through which we interpret the world. In fact, unknowingly we are living our life mostly on false beliefs. That's the main cause of many problems and unhappiness in our lives.

*Your **beliefs** become your thoughts. Your thoughts become your words. Your words become your actions. Your actions become your habits. Your habits become your values. Your values become your destiny.* — Mahatma Gandhi

For example, if you believe public speaking is terrifying, social events might become anxiety-inducing. Conversely, a belief in your own capabilities can propel you towards achieving seemingly impossible goals.

Checking the validity of belief:

There are several compelling reasons why checking the validity of your beliefs is important in designing your life:

False beliefs can lead you down the wrong path. Imagine believing "public speaking is a sign of weakness." This could prevent you from sharing your ideas, pursuing promotions, or even connecting with others on a deeper level. By checking the truth of your beliefs, you ensure your decisions are based on reality, increasing the chances of achieving your desired outcomes.

Limiting beliefs often fuel fear and anxiety. For example, the belief "failure is a disaster" can make you overly cautious, hindering your willingness to take risks or learn from mistakes. Questioning the validity of such beliefs can free you from unnecessary fear and open doors to new possibilities.

As shown in the diagram people have confined themselves in a limited materialistic world like a chick trapped in an eggshell. By designing your life, you will break free from limiting belief and will be exposed to an infinite psychological and spiritual world.

Break free from Limiting Beliefs

Finite Material World   **Infinite Psycho-Spiritual World**

Evaluating your beliefs fosters self-awareness. By uncovering the assumptions that drive your thoughts and actions, you gain a deeper understanding of who you are and what truly motivates you. This self-knowledge is essential for making conscious choices that align with your values and goals.

True beliefs are flexible and can adapt as you learn and grow. Holding onto demonstrably false beliefs makes you resistant to new information and experiences. Questioning your beliefs allows you to embrace a growth mindset, constantly seeking knowledge and evolving into the best version of yourself.

Empowering beliefs: by checking the validity of your beliefs, you take control of your own narrative. You can replace limiting beliefs with empowering ones, shaping your thoughts, emotions, and actions in a way that propels you towards your desired life.

In essence, checking the truth of your beliefs is about aligning your internal compass with reality. This ensures you're making informed decisions, acting with confidence, and ultimately, designing a life that reflects your true potential.

How to check whether your belief is true or false? This can be done by using the Shreyas and Preyas model advised by Lord of Death-Yamraj in Vedantic scripture Kath Upanishad. The concept is briefly described here:

Shreyas vs. Preyas: The Compass for Beliefs

Katha Upanishad, offers a powerful framework for evaluating beliefs – the concept of Shreyas and Preyas.

- **Shreyas** represents the ultimate good, the path leading to long-term well-being and fulfillment.
- **Preyas**, on the other hand, signifies the pleasurable, the seemingly attractive option that might bring immediate gratification but ultimately hinders your growth.

Yamraj, the Lord of Death, uses this concept to guide a young seeker. Imagine yourself in that role, with Yamraj presenting you with a choice: a delicious, tempting cake (Preyas) and a nourishing, healthy meal (Shreyas). Wise people chose Shreyas and unwise people go for Preyas.

Applying Shreyas and Preyas to Belief Evaluation

Here's how you can leverage this model to assess your own beliefs:

1. **Consider the Long-Term:** While a limiting belief like "I'm not good at public speaking" might seem to protect you from uncomfortable situations, ask yourself: Does it ultimately serve my goals? Would believing in my ability to improve as a speaker open door to greater opportunities?

2. **Think Consequences:** Explore the potential outcomes of your belief. Does it lead to personal growth, positive relationships, and a fulfilling life (Shreyas)? Or does it breed fear, stagnation, and missed opportunities (Preyas)?

3. **Align with Your Values:** Your core values are the guiding principles for your life. Does your belief align with those values, or does it contradict them?

Remember, Shreyas and Preyas are not absolutes. Sometimes, indulging in a "Preyas" experience can be a temporary reward on your journey towards "Shreyas." The key is to be mindful and ensure that the "Pleasurable" doesn't become a roadblock to the "Ultimately Good."

By incorporating this framework into your belief evaluation, you gain a powerful tool to discern beliefs that empower your life design from those that hold you back.

This is why, in designing your life, understanding and potentially reframing your beliefs becomes crucial.

Reframing Your Beliefs: a path to transformation

Reframing a belief is essentially revising the lens through which you see the world. It's about acknowledging existing beliefs, questioning their validity, and adopting new perspectives that better serve your goals.

Here's a roadmap to guide you through this process:

1. **Identify Your Beliefs:** Start by reflecting on your life patterns. What limiting beliefs might be holding you back? Are there fears that consistently prevent you from taking action? Journaling prompts like "What are my biggest fears?" or "What stories do I tell myself about success?" can be powerful tools for uncovering these hidden beliefs.

2. **Challenge the Narrative:** Once you've identified a belief, don't accept it at face value. Ask yourself: Is there evidence to support this belief? Are there alternative explanations for my experiences?

3. **Seek New Information:** Expose yourself to ideas and experiences that challenge your existing beliefs. Read books on personal development, attend workshops, or simply have conversations with people who hold different perspectives.

4. **Embrace New Possibilities:** As you gather evidence against your limiting beliefs, open yourself to the possibility of adopting new ones. What empowering belief could take its place?

5. **Take Action:** Beliefs are reinforced through action. Start small by taking steps that embody your new

belief. The more you act in accordance with your desired reality, the stronger your new belief becomes.

Remember, reframing is not a linear process. There will be setbacks and moments of doubt. But with consistent effort you can reshape your belief system and use it to design a life that aligns with your deepest aspirations.

By acknowledging the power of beliefs and actively reframing them, you unlock the potential to transform your story and design a life that truly reflects who you want to be.

5.2 Design Your Life

Imagine a life filled with purpose, fulfilment, and happiness. What would that look like for you? To develop a roadmap get you there, you are going to Design Your Life using the following six phases in twelve steps:

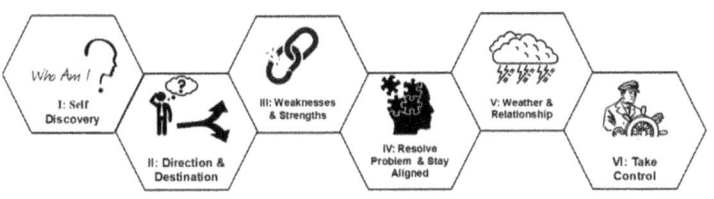

Design Your Life

Phase I: Self-Discovery
- **Discover Your Identity** (Sailboat): Unveil your true self and understand the essence of who you are.
- **Assess Your Present State** (Pathway): Evaluate where you stand in life at this moment.

Phase II: Direction & Destination of Life
- **Set Your Direction** (Steering): Determine the path you want to take guided by your values and aspirations.

- **Define Your Goals** (Destination): Establish clear objectives and milestones to strive for on your life's journey

Phase III: Personal Weaknesses & Strengths
- **Identify Your Weaknesses** (Leaks): Identify and mend personal weaknesses that impede your progress.
- **Enhance Your Personal Strengths** (Sails): Develop and harness your strengths to propel you forward and overcome obstacles.

Phase IV: Resolve Challenges and Staying Aligned
- **Resolve Challenges** (Repairs): Tackle life's hurdles head-on through problem-solving and resilience.
- **Stay Aligned** (Compass): Continuously monitor your journey, ensuring alignment with your values and goals

Phase V: Navigate Weathers & People Around
- **Navigate Stormy Times** (Weather): Adapt and persevere through life's unpredictable challenges and setbacks.
- **Cultivate Relationships** (Other Boats): Foster meaningful connections with those around you to enrich your journey

Phase VI: Take Control of Your Destiny
- **Embrace Your Role** (Captain): Take charge as the captain of your life, making intentional choices to shape your destiny.
- **Develop Odyssey Plan**: Make an action plan for improving your life over next five years.

The above phases and steps are described in detail in the coming chapters.

***

Chapter 6
Self-Discovery

The phase of self-discovery embarks your journey towards understanding yourself at a deeper level, unveiling the layers of your identity, and gaining clarity about your true essence.

This phase is characterized by introspection, reflection, and exploration of your beliefs, values, passions, strengths, and weaknesses. It's about delving into the core of who you are, uncovering your unique traits, desires, and motivations, and gaining insight into what makes you tick.

Self-discovery involves embracing authenticity and vulnerability, allowing yourself to be truly seen and understood, both by yourself and by others. It's about letting go of societal expectations, external influences, and past conditioning to uncover the authentic essence of your being.

Through self-discovery, you cultivate a deep sense of self-awareness and self-acceptance, learning to embrace all facets of your identity, including your strengths, quirks, and imperfections. This newfound understanding of yourself serves as a solid foundation for personal growth, empowerment, and living a life that is aligned with your true values and aspirations.

Ultimately, self-discovery is a continuous journey of exploration and self-awareness, a process of peeling back the layers of conditioning and societal expectations to reveal the authentic essence of who you are. It's about embracing your uniqueness, celebrating your individuality, and honouring the journey of becoming the most authentic version of yourself.

- Step 1: Discover Your Identity (Sailboat): Unveil your true self and understand the essence of who you are.
- Step 2: Assess Your Present State (Pathway): Evaluate where you stand in life at this moment

Step1: Discover Your Identity

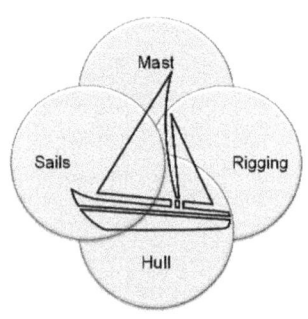

Constituents of Sailboat

Unveil your true self and understand the essence of who you are: In the sailboat metaphor, the "sailboat" represents the primal entity embarking on its journey across the vast ocean. Just as the sailboat comprises various components like the hull, mast, sails, and rigging for navigation, you, too, traverse the ocean of life amidst the physical world. To "Design Your Life," the crucial first step lies in recognizing who you are, not merely your physical form, but delving into your innermost being.

Every individual is endowed with four intrinsic and fundamental facets of personality: body, mind, intellect, and spirit. These components akin to the sailboat, form the vessel through which you navigate existence, each facet playing a distinct and complementary role in shaping your life's journey.

- **Body:** Your physical form is the vessel through which you navigate the material world. It serves as a vehicle for action, expression, and sensory experience, allowing you to interact with the physical realm and engage with the richness of the senses.

- **Mind:** The mind is the feeler, the seat of your emotions, and perceptions. It is a vast landscape of consciousness, where ideas take root, emotions blossom, and memories are etched into the fabric of your being. Through the power of the mind, you shape your reality and cultivate awareness of the world around you.

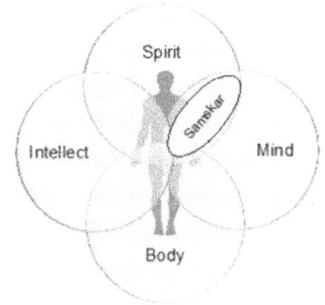

Constituents of Human Personality

- **Intellect:** The intellect is thinker, faculty of knowledge, discernment, wisdom, and higher understanding. It is through the intellect that you navigate the complexities of life, solve problems, making choices guided by principles of truth, ethics, and morality. The intellect serves as a guiding light, illuminating the path towards greater clarity and insight.

- **Spirit:** At the heart of your being resides the spirit- the sentient force, the eternal essence that transcends the confines of time and space. It is the divine energy that vitalizes your existence, makes your body, mind and intellect exist and function in this world, connecting you to the vastness of the universe and the source of all creation.

In fact, the real and only source of true happiness is the spirit. But, majority of people are ignorant about it and not consciously connected with their soul, that may be one of the root-causes of unhappiness in life. The spirit is the wellspring of your deepest aspirations, the inner compass that guides you towards your true purpose in life.

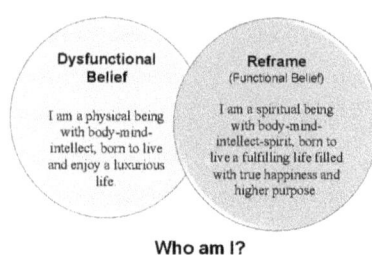

Who am I?

The function of your mind and intellect is influenced by a unique natural software called as "samskara".

Samskaras: The latent impressions or imprints left on the mind from past actions, experiences, and conditioning are samskaras. These imprints influence an individual's thoughts, emotions, habits, and behavior, shaping their personality, values, and aspirations in life. Based on your past karma you may be having positive or negative samskaras. Positive samskaras lead to virtuous actions and holistic growth, while negative samskaras result in ego-driven selfish actions and suffering. Example of some typical tendencies, evolved from samskaras are presented here:

Samskaras	
#	**Negative Tendencies**	**Positive Tendencies**
1	**Disorganization and Lack of Structure:** • Struggles to maintain order and structure in daily life. • Chaos and clutter characterize living spaces and schedules	**Embracing Structure and Organization:** • Follows order and efficiency in daily routines and environments. • Finds peace and productivity in a well-structured life

2	**Resistance to Physical Activity:**	**Prioritizing Physical Health and Wellbeing:**
	• Views exercise as discomfort rather than a means to nurture the body. • Finds excuses to avoid physical exertion.	• Practicing regular exercise for physical and mental health. • Loves physical activity as a source of vitality and rejuvenation.
3	**Preference for Unhealthy Eating Habits:**	**Embracing Nutritious Eating Habits:**
	• Prefers tasty and selective foods, ignores nutritional value. • Often indulges in unhealthy eating habits despite knowing the consequences.	• Chooses foods that nourish and sustain the body, prioritizing health over taste. • Appreciates the connection between diet and overall well-being.
4	**Pessimism and Fault-Finding:**	**Optimism and Positivity:**
	• Habitually focuses on flaws and shortcomings in people, situations, or oneself. • Sees the glass as half-empty rather than half-full.	• Cultivates a positive outlook, focusing on opportunities and solutions rather than problems. • Sees the beauty and potential for growth in every situation.
5	**Strong Biases and Judgmental Attitudes:**	**Open-Mindedness and Acceptance:**
	• Holds strong likes or dislikes towards specific individuals without rational basis. • Quickly judges others without considering diverse perspectives.	• Approaches people and situations with curiosity and acceptance, free from bias or prejudice. • Values diversity and seeks to understand different perspectives
6	**Constant Complaining and Negativity:**	**Gratitude and Contentment:**
	• Frequently complains about various aspects of life, including natural weather conditions.	• Expresses gratitude for life's blessings and finds joy in simple pleasures.

	• Tends to dwell on negative aspects rather than appreciating positives.	• Appreciates the present moment without constantly longing for more.
7	**Lack of Engagement and Easily Bored:** • Struggles to find fulfilment and interest in activities, leading to boredom. • Easily loses focus and interest in tasks or hobbies.	**Engagement and Curiosity:** • Maintains a sense of happiness and curiosity, in various activities and experiences. • Constantly seeks to learn and grow intellectually, emotionally, and spiritually
8	**Perception of Work as Burdensome:** • Views work as a burden rather than an opportunity for growth and contribution. • Lacks enthusiasm and motivation in professional endeavours	**Finding Purpose and Fulfilment in Work:** • Views work as a meaningful endeavour aligned with personal values and passions. • Finds fulfilment and purpose in making a positive impact through professional endeavours.
9	**Blame-Shifting and Avoidance of Responsibility:** • Avoids taking ownership of mistakes and failures, preferring to blame others. • Reluctant to face consequences or make amends for errors.	**Accountability and Integrity:** • Takes responsibility for actions and decisions, learning from mistakes and striving for improvement. • Values honesty and integrity in all interactions and endeavours
10	**Perfectionist Standards and Unrealistic Expectations:** • Sets unattainably high standards for oneself and others. • Expects perfection in every aspect of life, leading to dissatisfaction and stress.	**Balanced Standards and Realistic Expectations:** • Sets achievable goals and standards while maintaining a healthy balance between ambition and contentment. • Understands that perfection is unrealistic and embraces progress over perfection.
11	**Sense of Superiority and Entitlement:**	**Empathy and Humility:**

	• Holds an inflated sense of self-importance and superiority over others. • Expects special treatment and privileges without earning them.	• Empathizes with others' experiences and perspectives, fostering connection and understanding. • Approaches interactions with humility, recognizing one's own limitations and valuing the contributions of others.
12	**Materialism as a Means of Validation:** • Seeks validation and status through material possessions and visible consumption. • Buys things primarily to boost self-esteem or project a certain image to others	**Mindful Consumption and Purposeful Spending:** • Makes thoughtful choices when acquiring possessions, focusing on quality and utility rather than status. • Buys things with intention, considering their impact on personal well-being and the environment.

Determining who you are according to your samskaras involves deep introspection and self-awareness. Here are some steps you can take:

- **Self-reflection**: Spend time reflecting on your thoughts, emotions, and actions. Consider recurring patterns or habits in your life.

- **Identify your traits**: Reflect on your personality traits, such as introversion/extroversion, openness, conscientiousness, agreeableness, and emotional stability. Understanding your natural tendencies can help you understand yourself better.

- **Identify tendencies**: Notice your natural inclinations, strengths, weaknesses, likes, and dislikes. These can provide clues about your samskaras.

- **Self-assessment**: Take time to reflect on your values, beliefs, strengths, weaknesses, interests, and goals. Consider what motivates you and what brings you fulfilment.

Samskaras shape your Values and Beliefs

Samskaras are considered unconscious impressions or tendencies left behind by past experiences and actions. These can be positive (like a natural inclination towards compassion) or negative (like a fear of public speaking). They can act as a starting point for your values and beliefs.

- **Shaping Values:** Your natural tendencies (samskaras) can influence the values you develop. For instance, if you have a samskara for helping others, you might develop a strong value of compassion.

- **Influencing Beliefs:** Your samskaras can also colour your beliefs. Someone with a natural tendency towards leadership might believe they have a responsibility to take charge, while someone with a shyness samskara might believe they're not suited for leadership roles.

Understanding your samskaras is valuable for life design because they can be both a foundation and a potential obstacle. By recognizing your natural tendencies, you can leverage your positive samskaras to align with your values and challenge any limiting beliefs based on negative ones.

Ultimately, the journey of life with self-discovery involves understanding the nature of your personality and samskaras. And how samskaras influence shaping of your values and beliefs, which are your true identity. Through self-awareness and conscious effort, individuals can transcend the influence of samskaras and cultivate positive qualities such as gratitude, selflessness, and wisdom. Embrace the journey with an open heart and a committed spirit, knowing that every wave, every wind, and every moment carries the opportunity for growth, transcendence, and happiness.

> **Exercise:** Reflect on your personality traits and identify your present samskaras. Figure out what present tendencies you must change to attain success in life and wellbeing.

Step 2: Assess Your Present State

Evaluate where you stand in life at this moment: After knowing yourself, the next step is to know where you are now on your life pathway. Unless you know your present state, you can't know where are you going.

In the sailboat metaphor, the sailboat performs its journey on the water pathway of the vast ocean, similarly your life is performing its journey on four domains, which are the pathways of your life in the vast physical world.

Four domains of Life: The four natural constituents of your personality: body, mind, intellect, and spirit, each of them is having unique characteristic and function. To facilitate design, life is classified into four distinct domains as: physical life, family life, work life, and spiritual life representing four pathways on which your life is moving to attain its ultimate purpose. According to *Vedas*, the desired outcome of all actions in all domains of life is to seek happiness, which is the ultimate destination.

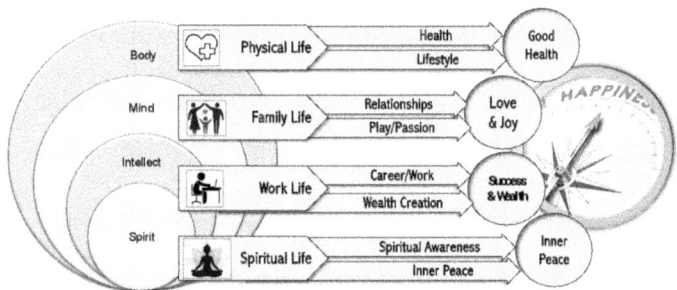

Domains and Pathways of Life

As such, life is considered as a complex philosophy. To make an objective assessment of present state of life journey in a quantitative way, each domain is subdivided into two parameters as key performance indicators (KPI), as shown in the table.

*	#	KPI (Parameters)	Assessment Criteria	Rating
Physical	1	Health	• Disease-free body, Physical fitness	
Physical	2	Lifestyle	• Daily routine as per nature, Balanced Diet, Exercise	
Family	3	Relationships	• Good relationships with parents, spouse, children, others	
Family	4	Play/Passion	• Play/Passion activities what makes you happy,	
Work	5	Career/Work	• Career growth, Competence, Job satisfaction	
Work	6	Wealth Creation	• Financial earnings from Work/Business	
Spiritual	7	Self Awareness	• Knowledge of the Self, Association with spiritual Institutions	
Spiritual	8	Inner Peace	• Yoga & Meditation practice. Agitation free mind.	

Life Assessment – Present State

Each key performance indicator of life is assessed against specific criteria, evaluated in terms of percent (%) accomplished, out of desired goal (100%), and shown in the life dashboard.

Self-Discovery

Life Dashboard											Where you are today?
Health ☹	10	20	30	40	50	60	70	80	90	100%	☺
Lifestyle											
Relationship											
Play											
Career											
Wealth											
Spiritual											
Inner Peace											
	Present Rating					Where you want to be in next 5 years					

Know the Gap: The gap between where you are (present state), and where want to be (future state) on all parameters are real challenge, which must be resolved to attain the goals of life.

For example; The life dash board of Ramesh, indicates the current rating of his health KPI 50% on the physical life pathway. It indicates that present health of Ramesh is not good, and is a major area of concern, he must take actions to improve health.

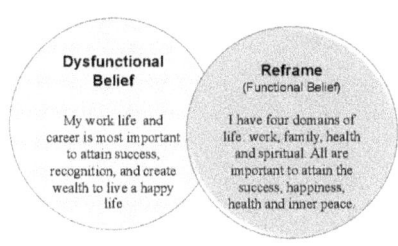

Domains of my Life

Present state assessment will enable you to identify the gap between your desired life (goal) and present life (actual). The quantum of gap indicates the severity of the problem of your life in the specific area, higher the gap bigger the concern. The present problems of each KPI are identified that must be resolved to live a happy life.

Make true assessment of present state of your life to know, where you are? Identify the gaps (current problems) of all eight parameters of your life. The present state assessment provides the baseline information to design your life, and plan actions for improvement.

	Life Assessment – Present State Problems			
*	#	KPI (Parameters)	Rating	GAP	Current problems of your Life
Physical	1	Health			
Physical	2	Lifestyle			
Family	3	Relationships			
Family	4	Play/Passion			
Work	5	Career/Work			
Work	6	Wealth Creation			
Spiritual	7	Self Awareness			
Spiritual	8	Inner Peace			

Exercise: Reflect on the concept, and make a self-assessment of your present state of all KPIs, and identify the problems of each area. Prepare a detailed list of all problems of your life. This is the most important step to design and improve your life.

***

Chapter 7
Direction & Destination of Life

This pivotal phase lays the groundwork for your life's journey, guiding you in defining the direction you wish to pursue and the destination you aim to reach.

Direction involves clarifying your life's purpose, values, and aspirations. It's about reflecting on what truly matters to you, what ignites your passion, and what drives you forward. By understanding your core values and envisioning the life you want to create, you set a clear direction for yourself, guiding your choices and actions towards a meaningful and fulfilling path.

Destination is about translating your aspirations into concrete goals and objectives. It's about identifying specific milestones and achievements that signify progress along your journey. By defining your destination, you create a roadmap that outlines the steps you need to take to turn your vision into reality, providing you with a sense of purpose and direction as you navigate through life's twists and turns.

Together, setting direction and defining destination empower you to embark on your life's journey with clarity, purpose, and intention. By aligning your actions with your values and aspirations and setting clear goals to strive for, you create a roadmap that guides you towards a future that is truly fulfilling and rewarding.

- Step 3: Set Direction of your Life (Steering): Determine the path you want to take guided by your values and aspirations.

- Step 4: Define Your Goals (Destination): Establish clear objectives and milestones to strive for on your life's journey.

Step 3: Set Direction of Your Life

Determine the path you want to take: The sailboat moves on water pathway; to reach destination it must move in the right direction. The direction of the sailboat is determined by the steering, according to the sailing plan. Similarly, direction of your life is determined by your personal values - what is most important to you, and life and work views. Your present values function as steering of your life.

To design your life, you must first understand yourself, your needs, aspirations, and present problems, by reflecting and getting answers to the following fundamental questions:

- **Identity:** what are your personal values?
- **Life view:** what kind of life you dream and aspire to live?
- **Work view:** what is your approach to work and career aspirations?

When you connect all three together in a logical way, you may start to experience your life as meaningful.

Personal Values: Values are considered as the core element of a person's life. Anything that is most important to you in your life is called value. Personal values are the fundamental beliefs and principles that guide an individual's behavior, decisions, actions, and interactions with others. Value serves as a moral compass, influencing how individuals prioritize their actions and navigate life.

Values provide individuals, a sense of direction and purpose in life. Values shape ethical conduct, interpersonal relationships, and societal engagement. When individuals prioritize values such as honesty, respect, compassion, and justice, they contribute to a culture of trust, cooperation, and mutual respect.

Values reflect an individual's identity and character. They define who a person is, and what they stand for, serving as a foundation for self-expression and authenticity. By living in alignment with their values, individuals express their true selves and cultivate a sense of integrity and self-respect. Values can provide a source of strength and resilience during challenging times. They offer a sense of meaning and purpose, helping individuals navigate adversity and maintain a sense of hope and optimism. Living in accordance with one's values contributes to psychological well-being and inner satisfaction.

Personal values are deeply ingrained and often evolve from a combination of genetics (as *samskara-* the subtle effects of your past *karma*), upbringing, culture, learning, experiences, and reflections on what is meaningful and important to oneself. While values are considered core elements of a person's life, it's important to recognize that they may vary from one individual to another based on cultural, religious, familial, and personal influences. What matters most is that individuals consciously reflect on their values, strive to live in alignment with them, and foster an environment that honours and respects diverse perspectives and beliefs.

Your present values may be positive (adaptive) or negative (nonadaptive). Positive values contribute to well-being, while negative values reduce wellbeing and happiness. Your values determine the direction of your life. Some of the most common positive values that help to "moving toward" towards the goals of life:

Positive Values		
Values	*Description*	*Priority*
Honesty	Being truthful and sincere in interactions with others promotes trust and integrity.	
Kindness	Showing compassion, empathy, and generosity towards others	
Respect	Treating others with consideration, dignity, and fairness.	
Integrity	Being honest, truthful, and principled in all dealings.	
Gratitude	Appreciating and expressing thankfulness for the blessings and kindness received.	
Courage	Facing challenges, adversity, and fears with strength and resilience.	
Empathy	Understanding and sharing the feelings and perspectives of others	
Perseverance	Persisting in the pursuit of goals despite obstacles or setbacks.	
Humility	Recognizing one's strengths and limitations without arrogance or pride	
Optimism	Maintaining a positive outlook and mindset, even in difficult circumstances	

The negative values that make you "moving away" from the goals of life. To attain success and happiness, you need to identify your negative values and replace them with positive values according to your goals. Some of the most common negative values are presented here:

Negative Values		
Values	*Description*	*Priority*
Dishonesty	Engaging in deceitful or manipulative behaviour.	
Selfishness	Prioritizing one's own needs and desires at the expense of others	
Violence	Inflicting harm or suffering on others intentionally or callously	
Arrogance	Displaying an excessive sense of superiority or entitlement	
Prejudice	Holding biased or discriminatory attitudes toward individuals or groups	
Ingratitude	Failing to appreciate or acknowledge the efforts and kindness of others	
Cowardice	Avoiding challenges or difficult situations out of fear or weakness	
Indifference	Showing apathy or lack of concern towards the feelings or needs of others	
Pessimism	Adopting a negative outlook and mindset, expecting failure or disappointment	
Rigidity	Being inflexible or closed-minded in beliefs or attitudes	

Life View: To design your life, it's important to visualize what kind of life you dream and aspire to live, is expressed as a "Life View". As the captain of your life, you must know what kind of journey you wish to perform in life. By developing a clear life view, you can steer your life in the direction you desire, guided by your values to attain the goals while navigating the various challenges and opportunities that come your way. Your life view represents your understanding of yourself, your values, your goals, and the external factors that may influence your journey. Personal values define what is most important to you in your life, and determine the direction of your life journey. Destinations indicate the ultimate purpose and goals related to your physical, family, professional, and spiritual lives. Identifying your strengths, weaknesses, preferences, competencies, and resources is essential for effective navigation of life. Awareness of the external environment, people, social conditions, and favorable and adverse situations you may come across in your life journey is very important.

Example of life view of Ramesh, a corporate manager. "My life view is rooted in a clear vision of the kind of life I dream and aspire to live, shaped by my personal values, goals, and aspirations. I understand the importance of visualizing my desired destinations across the physical, family, professional, and spiritual aspects of my life.

Central to my life view is a deep understanding of myself - my strengths, weaknesses, preferences, and competencies. By harnessing these insights, I can navigate my life with confidence and purpose, leveraging my resources to overcome challenges and seize opportunities along the way. Additionally, I remain keenly aware of the external environment, recognizing the influence of people, social conditions, and changing circumstances on my journey. In my life, I give due importance to my family by spending quality time with them an ensuring that life is made interesting by spending vacations at pleasing natural and interesting places of the world.

On my life journey, I am guided by my values, which serve as the North Star illuminating my path. With a clear life view as my compass, I am empowered to steer towards my desired destinations, embracing the adventure of life with courage, resilience, and purpose."

Work View: The "work view" represents your perspective on work and career within the broader context of your life journey. Your work view focuses specifically on your approach to work, professional fulfilment, and career aspirations. Your work view involves identifying your career goals and aspirations. Knowledge and skills, expertise, and attitude required to progress in your career. External factors such as global and national economic conditions, industry trends, and job market can influence your career like wind affects the direction of the sailboat. Your work view must be integrated with your life goals, values, priorities, well-being, and aspirations. While career success is important for financial growth, it's essential to ensure that your career balances your work, family, and personal, spiritual life to achieve long-term success, job satisfaction, meaningful life, and happiness.

Example work view of Ramesh: My work view is deeply integrated with my life journey, reflecting a holistic approach to career fulfilment and personal well-being. I see my career as a vital component of my life, aligned with my values, aspirations, and priorities. Central to this perspective is the pursuit of meaningful contribution, continuous learning, and collaboration in the professional realm.

I recognize the importance of setting clear career goals and aspirations, grounded in a solid foundation of knowledge, skills, and expertise. I am committed to ongoing education, training, and skill development to stay relevant and adaptable in a rapidly evolving landscape. Additionally, I value maintaining a proactive attitude, embracing challenges as opportunities for growth and advancement.

I am mindful of global and national economic conditions, industry trends, and job market dynamics, which may influence my career. By staying informed, I can effectively assess and respond to these factors, charting a course that maximizes opportunities and minimizes risks.

Importantly, I view career success not in isolation but as part of a balanced life that encompasses work, family, and personal well-being. While financial growth is a consideration, it is equally essential to prioritize the integration of work and personal life to achieve long-term satisfaction, fulfilment, and happiness.

Direction of Life

The direction of life depends on the type of personal values embraced by you in your journey. What values will guide you to follow the right path and accomplish life goals is explained in one of the classical spiritual scriptures- *Katha Upanishad*, according to that lord of death-*Yamaraj* imparted the supreme knowledge to an young seeker Nachiketa. In the context of the direction of life, the Katha Upanishad suggests that individuals have to choose any one of the two paths: Shreyas (good) or Preyas (pleasant) to navigate their lives and pursue their goals. These two directions are briefly explained here;

- ***Shreyas* (Good):** *Shreyas,* refers to the path of the good or the noble. It involves choosing actions and pursuits that lead to long-term well-being, spiritual growth, enlightenment, and holistic prosperity. Shreyas involves seeking the higher truths of existence and aligning one's actions with values of righteousness, virtue, and selflessness. It emphasizes the pursuit of knowledge, wisdom, and inner fulfilment, even if it involves sacrifice or hardship in the short term.

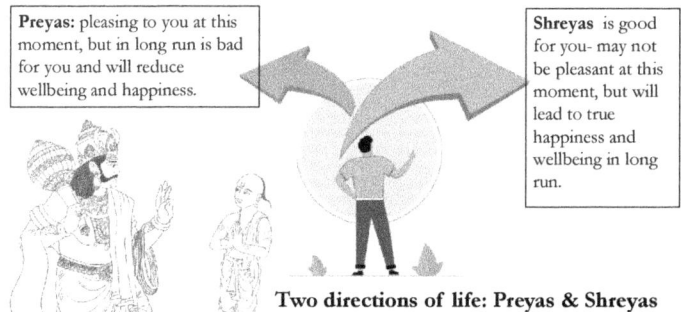

Two directions of life: Preyas & Shreyas

- *Preyas* **(Pleasant)**: *Preyas*, on the other hand, refers to that which is pleasant or enjoyable. It involves choosing actions and pursuits that bring immediate pleasure, gratification, or worldly success. Preyas focuses on fulfilling selfish desires, pursuing material comforts, seeking external validation and pleasure. While *Preyas* may offer immediate gratification, it often leads to temporary happiness, attachment, and dependence on external sources for fulfilment. Preyas is often associated with the path of materialism and pleasure-seeking.

Choosing Preyas may lead to momentary pleasures and worldly achievements, but may ultimately result in dissatisfaction, attachment, and spiritual ignorance. On the other hand, choosing Shreyas involves prioritizing spiritual growth, ethical conduct, and inner fulfilment over temporary pleasures or worldly success.

The path of Shreyas always wins, even when it appears to lose, and the path of Preyas is a loser's path, even when it appears to be winning. The Katha Upanishad encourages individuals to reflect on the consequences of their actions and to choose the path of Shreyas for lasting happiness and fulfilment. The wise men choose out the Shreyas from the Preyas, but the dull-witted chooses the pleasant.

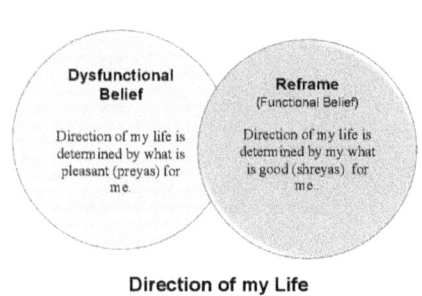

Direction of my Life

Due to ignorance of this concept and influence of materialism, the majority of people choose the path of Preyas for instant gratification, which is one of the major causes of unhappiness.

Preyas- Shreyas a decision-making tool:

During the lifetime, at work place or in personal life everyone has to take several decisions to select a choice out of many options. Most of the time, based on their likes and limited knowledge people go for the Preyas, which may prove wrong in long-term. Whenever you are in dilemma, use the Preyas-Shreyas concept to take a right decision using the following

Preyas- Shreyas Decision Making Tool (Beneficiaries of Decision)								
Decision Options	Me	My Family	My Company	My Customer	Society/ Country	Mother Nature	Type of Decision	My Decision
1	✓	✗	✗	✗	✗	✗	Win-Lose	Preyas
2	✓	✓	✗	✗	✗	✗	Win-Lose	Preyas
3	✓	✓	✓	✓	✗	✗	Win-Lose	Preyas
4	✓	✓	✓	✓	✓	✓	Win-Win	Shreyas

reflection, and conscious decision-making. By aligning values with higher principles and long-term well-being, individuals can cultivate a sense of purpose, fulfilment, and physical, emotional, intellectual, and spiritual growth in their lives.

How to control the direction of your life?

The current direction of your life is guided by your present values. If you are not happy, it means that the direction of your life is not aligned with your values or you are following Preyas values. By changing your values, you can steer your life in a new direction, toward a destination that aligns more closely with your desires and aspirations.

Visualize your life as a sailboat traveling in the vast ocean, and the values you hold are the wind that propels the sails of the sailboat to move forward. Direction of the sailboat is set and controlled by the steering. Similarly, you can change direction of your life by changing your values in the following way:

- **Assess your current direction**: Are you sailing toward the desired destination? Check whether your values align with this direction. If not, it's time for a course correction.

- **Identify your present values**: In the case of a sailboat, the values you hold are like the wind, the direction of the wind decides the sailboat's direction, similarly your present value determines the direction of your life, whether helping you to move in the right direction.

- **Change your values**: Determine your desired destination and life goals. Reconfirm your present values, and make a conscious effort to change the present values like adjusting your sails in the sailboat.

  For example, if you value relaxation over exercise, but your life goal is good health, then you need to change your value to exercise over relaxation. Changing the value is not so easy, there may be internal resistance, which you have to overcome and adapt.

- **Enjoy the Journey**: Life journey is not just about reaching the destination or achieving the goals only. The ultimate purpose of life is enjoying every moment of the journey and embracing the ups and downs, the challenges and victories, as you sail towards your goals.

> **Exercise:** Reflect and identify your current positive and negative values. What negative values you want to change? Develop your life view and work view. Check the direction of your life.

Step 4: Define Your Goals

Establish clear objectives and milestones for your life's journey: In the sailboat metaphor "destination" represents the objective or goals of life, the ultimate vision, where you want to go. At the same time, it is important to know the pathways and waypoints (milestones) of your journey to reach the destination. Without knowing the destination (goals) and waypoints the sailboat is likely to be lost in the sea, exposed to all sorts of danger, and at the risk of damage or sinking. Similarly in life, if you don't have clear goals and milestones, you don't know where will you land?

Stages of Life: As per Upanishads, the journey of human life moves forward through four distinct stages along with increasing age; Brahmacharya, Grihastha, Vanaprastha, and Sanyas, known as Ashramas. Every stage has specific needs and responsibilities for individuals.

The Four Stages of Life

Ashrama	Description
Brahmacharya (Student Life) Up to 25 Years Age	This stage typically begins with childhood and extends up to early adulthood. The primary focus is on education, character building, and the acquisition of knowledge. Students are expected to live a disciplined life with celibacy under the guidance of a Guru (teacher) in a Gurukul or similar educational setup. The emphasis is on learning the scriptures, acquiring professional skills, and cultivating virtues like humility, discipline, and truthfulness.
Grihastha (Householder & Work Life) +25 to 60 Years Age	This stage begins after completion of the student phase, typically with marriage. The focus shifts towards fulfilling societal and familial duties, including raising a family, pursuing a career, creating wealth, and contributing to society. Grihastha are expected to lead a balanced life, managing their responsibilities towards family, society, profession, and personal growth. It's also a time for spiritual growth through practicing Dharma (righteousness), Artha (material prosperity), Kama (sensual pleasures), and Moksha (liberation) within the confines of societal norms.
Vanaprastha (Retired Life) +60 to 75 Years Age	Vanaprastha marks the gradual withdrawal from active worldly pursuits and responsibilities. Typically beginning around middle age, individuals in this stage gradually detach themselves from material possessions and social obligations. The focus shifts towards spiritual practices, contemplation, and preparing for the eventual renunciation of worldly life. Vanaprastha often involves practice of meditation, study, and reflection, though this can also manifest as a simpler lifestyle. It's a period for deepening one's spiritual understanding, seeking liberation (Moksha), and imparting wisdom to younger generations.

| Sanyas
(Renunciate Life)
+75 Years Age	Sanyas is the final stage of life, marked by complete renunciation of worldly attachments and desires. Sanyasis (renunciates) devote themselves entirely to spiritual pursuits, detached from societal roles, possessions, and relationships. They lead a life of austerity, simplicity, and detachment, and focusing solely on attaining spiritual enlightenment and liberation.

These four stages provide a framework for individuals to lead a well-rounded life, balancing worldly responsibilities with spiritual growth. The underlying principles of self-discipline, duty, and spiritual evolution remain relevant for seekers of truth and fulfilment. In the present era, one of the main causes of miseries of people is not following the recommendations of ancient and validated wisdom. Due to materialistic thinking and spiritual ignorance, people hankering for infinite wealth and authority even after reaching very senior age. Scriptures recommend, to live a holistic and happy life every individual should follow the concept of Ashrama. These are equally relevant even today.

Goal setting and achievement are the most important processes to make a successful life journey. While setting the goals, based on your present age, the needs and responsibilities of four Ashrams may be taken into consideration. The goals can be short-term or long-term, specific or general, must be for all aspects of life; physical, family, work, and spiritual lives.

Two types of goals: There are two types of goals; the "end goal" and "means goal". End goal is what we aim to achieve, and means goals are what we use to do, what we aim to achieve.

Defining the end goal and means goals of life can vary greatly from person to person, as they are deeply personal and reflective of individual values, beliefs, and aspirations. Mostly, people are confused with means goal as the ultimate objective, and fail to achieve the real purpose. To facilitate realistic goal setting, a clear perspective of goals is given below:

End Goal: It refers to the final destination or result that one is striving for. In general, the ultimate goal of everyone's life is to seek happiness (*Anand*). The ultimate goal can be attained by setting and achieving the means goals.

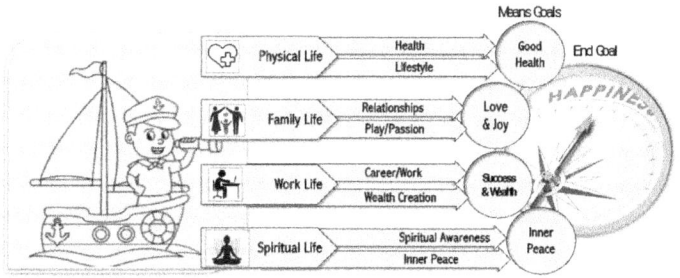

KPIs and Goals of Life

Means Goals: The means goals are steps you take to achieve your end goal. As explained life is functioning thorough four core domains; physical life, family life, work life, and spiritual life, each of them are further divided into two key performance indicators as per nature of life. The end goal of life - happiness can be achieved only by performing the necessary activities to achieve the means goals of all eight KPIs of physical, family, work, and spiritual lives. To attain the end goal, you must set the means goals for the following eight key performance indicators (means) of life:

1. **Health**: Your body is your real lifelong companion; it must be healthy. Health is the foundation of life, unless you are physically fit, you can't perform

correct actions and enjoy experiences of life. Health encompasses physical, mental, and emotional well-being. Prioritizing health ensures vitality, longevity, and resilience to diseases.

2. **Lifestyle:** Lifestyle refers to the way an individual lives, it includes their daily habits, routines, and activities. Lifestyle plays the most important role in maintaining good health. It involves maintaining a balanced diet, regular exercise, adequate sleep, and managing stress.

3. **Relationships**: Cultivating meaningful connections with family, friends, mentors, and colleagues that provide support, love, respect, and fulfilment. Healthy relationships are built on trust, respect, communication, and mutual support. Nurturing meaningful relationships fosters emotional intimacy, social support, and a sense of belonging.

4. **Play/Passion:** Play represents activities that bring joy, creativity, and spontaneity into life. It includes hobbies, sports, arts, music, travel, and other forms of recreation. Engaging in play promotes relaxation, stress relief, and stimulates creativity and imagination.

5. **Career/Work**: Career refers to one's professional pursuits. Career growth is an important outcome of professional success, which depends on personal initiative for knowledge and skill development, and engagement in work during work life. A fulfilling career provides financial stability, personal growth, and a sense of achievement

6. **Wealth creation:** Creating wealth to fulfil one's goals and aspirations is an important parameter of life. Wealth creation capability is also linked with competence and career growth. Building wealth provides security, opportunities for growth, and the ability to support oneself and others. To create wealth, you must have knowledge & skills of latest operational excellence techniques.

7. **Spiritual awareness**: Spiritual awareness entails connecting with one's inner self, higher consciousness, or transcendent reality. It involves practices such as learning spiritual concepts, and meditation. Cultivating spiritual awareness deepens one's understanding of life's purpose, meaning, and interconnectedness.

8. **Inner Peace:** Inner peace is a state of calmness, contentment, and harmony within oneself. It arises from acceptance, gratitude, forgiveness, and letting go of negativity. Cultivating inner peace fosters emotional resilience, mental clarity, and a sense of serenity amidst life's challenges.

Setting means goals for these eight parameters involve reflecting on life view, values, priorities, and aspirations. The goals should align with your vision of fulfilling life, while also allowing for flexibility and adaptation as circumstances change.

Measurable Goals: While goal setting, it is important to ensure that goals are specific, measurable, achievable, realistic, and time-bound (SMART) so that the ultimate objective of life is achieved with confidence and satisfaction. If goals are not measurable, it can't be effectively monitored and controlled. In case of life, it is quite challenging to fix key performance indicators and quantified goals. To make goals measurable, it is quantified as relative percentage of your highest expectations.

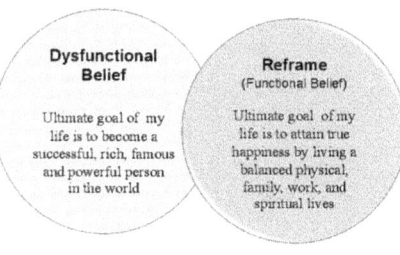

Destination of my Life

Goal Setting: Recognizing the rapidly changing conditions of life, means goals can be set for a short term of five year, and subsequently reiterated in future course. Goal setting is not only quantitative, but it should be subjective with clear description of what actions to be taken and outcome will be experienced after it is achieved. A typical criterion to facilitate goal setting is provided here;

Goal Setting for next 5 Years					
*	#	Parameters	Criteria	Present	Goal
Physical	1	Health	What and how much you want to improve your health?		
Physical	2	Lifestyle	What changes you will make in your lifestyle?		
Family	3	Relationships	Good relationships with parents, spouse, children, others		
Family	4	Play/Passion	Activities to make you and your family happy?		
Work	5	Career/Work	Competency development targets and growth in career?		
Work	6	Wealth Creation	Financial earning targets from Work/Business?		
Spiritual	7	Self Awareness	Actions to enhance your spiritual knowledge and awareness		
Spiritual	8	Inner Peace	Learning and practice of Yoga & Meditation?		

For example; During the present state self-assessment, a corporate manager Ramesh rated his present health at 50% of his own standard. To improve health, he has set a target to reach 70% level during the next five years, as shown in the life dashboard. His present rating of spiritual and inner peace parameters is practically negligible, this may be the cause of excessive materialistic desires and lack of mental peace, which might be adversely impacting his health also.

Life Dashboard — Means Goals — Where do you see yourself **5 years** from now?

Parameter	10	20	30	40	50	60	70	80	90	100%
Health										
Lifestyle										
Relationship										
Play										
Career										
Wealth										
Spiritual										
Inner Peace										

Present Rating ▓ Goals for the next 5 years

To make an additional 20% improvement in health from the present level, Ramesh has to identify the problems which are preventing him to reach the 70% target. On the spiritual front, to improve his wellbeing and enjoy life, Ramesh must take initiatives to improve spiritual awareness and inner peace.

	Problems to be Solved to attain the Goals				
	KPIs	Present	Goal	Gap	Problems
1	Health				
2	Lifestyle				
3	Relationships				
4	Play/Passion				
5	Career/Work				
6	Wealth Creation				
7	Self Awareness				
8	Inner Peace				

The similar exercises done to set goals and identify the problems of all eight parameters. Based on the importance and urgency, problems are prioritized, and solved to reach the goals. Problem solving is discussed in step-7: resolve problems.

Goal setting activity not only setting the targets, but helping to discover the actual problems of life hindering progress and setting agenda to address. This is a crucial step to "design your life" and move forward in life journey.

> **Exercise:** On your life dashboard sheet, make a self-assessment of your present state of all 8 parameters of life, and set means goals for the next 5 years and identify problems.

***

Chapter 8
Personal Weaknesses & Strengths

This phase is centred around self-improvement and personal growth, focusing on identifying and addressing areas for improvement while also nurturing and leveraging your inherent strengths.

Weaknesses involves recognizing and acknowledging areas of vulnerability or limitation within yourself. It's about embracing self-awareness and honesty to identify areas where you may be falling short or facing challenges. By acknowledging these weaknesses, you create an opportunity for growth and development, paving the way for personal transformation and improvement.

Strengths is about recognizing and harnessing your innate talents, abilities, and qualities. It's about nurturing and honing the areas where you excel, amplifying your strengths to their fullest potential. By investing time and effort into developing your strengths, you not only enhance your capabilities but also boost your confidence and resilience, empowering yourself to overcome obstacles and achieve success.

Together, addressing weaknesses and developing strengths create a balanced approach to self-improvement and personal development. By acknowledging and working on areas for improvement while also nurturing and leveraging your strengths, you cultivate a strong foundation for growth, resilience, and success in all aspects of your life.

- Step 5: Mend Your Weaknesses (Leaks): Identify and mend personal weaknesses that impede your progress.
- Step 6: Enhance Your Strengths (Sails): Develop and harness your strengths to propel you forward and overcome obstacles.

Step 5: Identify Your Weaknesses

Leaks in the Sailboat

Identify & mend your weaknesses hindering your progress: The leaks in the sailboat are something that retard the progress of the journey or may sink the boat, if it is not repaired in time. The "leaks" represent "personal weaknesses" or challenges that reduce your wellbeing and happiness in life. A weakness is anything that hinders proper functioning and retards growth, prevents living personal values and achieving goals, disturbs inner peace, and make you unhappy.

The leaks in a sailboat through some cracks or holes in hull allow water to seep in and potentially slow down or sink the vessel. Actions to fetch out the water, or plugging the leaks consume energy, efforts and time, hinders progress. The leaks occur due to some holes in the hull or deficiencies and capability of sails, masts, rigging or inefficient navigation of sailboat.

Similarly, leaks in your life appear as personal weaknesses in your personality resulting to wrong decisions, imperfect actions, mistakes and unpleasant behavior, that hamper growth and success in life. These leaks drain valuable energy, time, efforts and resources for rectification.

Personal weaknesses can be broadly classified as physical, psychological, intellectual, and spiritual types. Here are some common examples of personal weaknesses (leaks) that work as obstacles to progress and success in your life:

Personal Weaknesses		
Life Domain	Leaks (personal weaknesses)	Main Causes
Physical	Poor health, chronic disease, lack of stamina, undisciplined routine, lack of time management, lack of practical skills, no physical exercise, unhealthy diet, unhealthy habits, etc.	Wrong lifestyle
Psychological	Negative thoughts, ego, selfishness, anger, greed, fear of failure, frustration, procrastination, dishonesty, arrogance. Lack of motivation, no self-confidence, inconsistent behaviour, strong likes & dislikes, critical nature, lack of trust, revengeful nature, distrust. Materialism, perfectionism, social comparison, maximizing.	Negative attitude, Weakness focus
Intellectual	Inadequate knowledge & skills, Indecisiveness, lack of clarity, distraction, disengaged in duty, insincerity, irresponsibility, unplanned working, lack of communication and problem-solving skills, etc.	Incompetence, Fixed Mindset
Spiritual	Mental agitations, attachment, ego, worries, anxiety, fear. No spiritual awareness, no knowledge and practice of yoga and meditation, etc.	Spiritual Ignorance

When these weaknesses dominate individual behavior, they lead to negative emotions, disengagement at work, and a lack of motivation that prevents growth in life. When we adopt a weakness focus, we focus solely on the leaks. For example, in case when something wrong happens in our life, we focus on what is wrong with an individual or ourselves, instead of why it is wrong. We direct attention to the negative aspects of the person. In the context of professional activities and performance, a weak focus means that we are primarily concerned with behaviour that is causing suboptimal or poor performance.

The belief behind weakness focus is that; by fixing the weakness, you try to increase well-being and happiness. In terms of the sailboat metaphor, by fixing the leaks you expect the boat to be able to sail again. Indeed, if you do not fix the leak, then the boat may sink and the captain will not be able to sail anywhere.

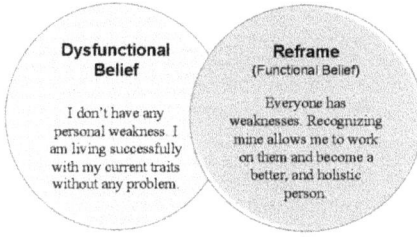

My Personal Weaknesses

However, aiming to increase well-being by only focusing on repairing the leak of the boat is unlikely to attain success. This approach ignores the fact that the absence of physical disease or problems in life does not automatically imply good health and happiness. Regarding the metaphor, even if you would be able to repair the leak, you may still not be able to get where you want to be.

Three most common Leaks: Majority of professionals have three most common leaks: Frustration, Fear, and Procrastination. These leaks reduce their performance, hinder progress in life, and develop unhappiness.

Frustration: *Breaking through the wall*

Adam, a graduate engineer joined a reputed public sector organization. A hard working and sincere engineer, dedicated to his profession. He was satisfied with his job, because he was able to apply his engineering knowledge very well. He was quite ambitious about his career, after few years of working, due to delays in his promotion he became frustrated, and started looking for new options. Despite of secured job and high degree of job satisfaction, he left the company and joined a reputed private sector organization.

Frustration is a common problem for most professionals working in employment secured organizations like public sectors and government. Frustration is like "leaks" in the sailboat, as personal weakness, demotivates, hinders the progress, and creates unhappiness in life.

Let us understand the causes of frustration and find out how to overcome this psychological "leak" and enhances happiness.

Frustration is a state of emotional tension caused by the inability to achieve a desired goal or by the presence of obstacles that prevent progress.

Frustration can arise from a perceived mismatch between your efforts and the desired outcome. This feeling can be accompanied by physiological changes like increased heart rate and muscle tension, as well as negative thoughts and behaviors like anger, irritability, or withdrawal.

Causes of Frustration

- **Feeling like a great contributor but not getting recognition or career growth:** This can be a common cause of frustration for people working in secured jobs, or any job where they feel their talents are not being fully utilized or not well recognized.

- **Lack of feeling secure:** Even in a secure job, people can feel frustrated if they don't feel secure in their role or their future with the company. This could be due to a lack of career growth, or a lack of clarity about what is expected of them in order to advance in their career.

- **Lack of control:** People who feel like they don't have control over their work or their careers are more likely to feel frustrated. This could be due to a micromanaging boss, or a lack of opportunities to take on new challenges.

How to Overcome Frustration

- **Identify the source of your frustration:** The first step to dealing with frustration is to figure out what's causing it. Once you know what the problem is, you can start to brainstorm solutions.

- **Communicate your needs:** If you're feeling frustrated because you're not getting the recognition you deserve, talk to your boss or supervisor. Let them know what you're hoping to achieve in your career, and ask for their feedback on how you can get there.

- **Take control of your career:** If you're feeling frustrated because you don't feel like you're in control of your career, start taking steps to change that. Look for opportunities to take on new challenges, or develop new skills. You can also start networking with people in your field, to learn about other opportunities.

- **Focus on the positive:** It's important to focus on the positive aspects of your job, even when you're feeling frustrated. What are you good at? What do you enjoy doing? Focusing on the positive can help to improve your overall mood and outlook.

- **Find a healthy outlet for your frustration:** If you're feeling frustrated, it's important to find a healthy way to express those feelings. Exercise, spending time in nature, or talking to a friend or therapist can all be helpful ways to cope with frustration.

By following these tips, you can learn to manage your frustration in a healthy way and create a more fulfilling career for yourself.

Fear: *A common challenge in the workplace*

Adam, after working in an organization with high job security, he shifted to a reputed private sector organization (highly unsecured job), at senior level with good package and benefits. Due to his technical competence and good interests in taking up new challenges, he could contribute well in new developments. But due to typical private sector culture, driven by the owners likes and dislikes, despite good competence and confidence in his capabilities, he lived with fear of uncertainties in the job.

Fear is an emotional response to a perceived threat or danger. Fear is an evolutionary response that helps us avoid potential harm. Fear is one of the most common psychological state experienced in most of the private sector organizations, irrespective of the level of the job and size of company.

Fear is a primal emotion that can hold us back from achieving our dreams. It is one of the major "leaks" or personal weakness of individual, reduces happiness. It triggers the fight-or-flight response, preparing our bodies to react quickly. Fear can be specific (e.g., fear of heights) or more general (e.g., social anxiety). While fear can be helpful in some situations, excessive or irrational fear can be debilitating. But in "Design Your Life," we're all about moving forward. Let's explore the causes of fear and equip ourselves with strategies to overcome them.

Causes of Workplace Fear

Fear is a common emotion experienced by many professionals, even those in high positions. The text mentions that fear can plague even highly competent and experienced persons. This fear can come from a number of sources, including:

- **Job Security:** The instability of the job market can cause fear, especially for those in private sector jobs where there may not be strong job security.

- **Performance Anxiety:** The fear of not being good enough, or of making mistakes, can be a significant source of workplace fear.

- **Lack of Control:** A feeling of helplessness or lack of control over one's work or career path can be very frightening.

Overcoming Workplace Fear

The good news is that fear can be managed. Here are some tips:

- **Identify the Source:** The first step to overcoming fear is to identify what's causing it. Once you understand the root of your fear, you can start to develop strategies to address it.

- **Focus on What You Can Control:** While some things may be outside your control, focus on the aspects of your work that you can influence. This can help you feel more empowered.

- **Develop Coping Mechanisms:** Everyone has different ways of dealing with fear. Find healthy coping mechanisms that work for you, such as exercise, relaxation techniques, or talking to a trusted friend or therapist.
- **Build Your Confidence:** The more confident you feel in your abilities, the less fear will have a hold on you.
- **Take Action:** Don't let fear paralyze you. Take small steps towards your goals, and celebrate your accomplishments along the way.

By following these tips, you can learn to manage workplace fear and create a more fulfilling career for yourself

Procrastination: *The thief of time*

Procrastination is the act of delaying or postponing a task or set of tasks. Procrastination is one of the quite common weaknesses of most people. Procrastination is a common problem that can hold people back from achieving their goals.

Causes of Procrastination

Procrastination often stems from a desire to avoid negative emotions associated with the task. There are many reasons why people procrastinate, but some of the most common include:

- **Fear of Failure:** People who are afraid of failing may put off starting a task because they are worried about not being successful.
- **Lack of Motivation:** If you don't feel motivated to do something, it's easy to put it off until later.

- **Perfectionism:** People who are perfectionists may procrastinate because they are afraid of not doing something perfectly.

- **A Big or Complicated Task:** A large or complex task can seem overwhelming, leading people to put it off until the last minute.

Overcoming Procrastination

There are a number of things you can do to overcome procrastination:

- **Break down large tasks into smaller, more manageable steps.** This will make the task seem less daunting and help you get started.

- **Set realistic deadlines for yourself.** Don't try to do too much at once.

- **Reward yourself for completing tasks.** This will help you stay motivated.

- Find a quiet place to work where you will not be interrupted.

- Let others know about your goals and ask them to hold you accountable.

- **Identify your triggers.** What are the things that make you more likely to procrastinate? Once you know your triggers, you can develop strategies to avoid them.

- **Start with the most important task.** This will help you to make the most of your time.

- **Eliminate distractions.** Turn off your phone and close unnecessary browser tabs.

- **Just get started.** Sometimes the hardest part is just beginning. Once you get started, you may find that the task is not as difficult as you thought

By following the above tips, you can learn to overcome procrastination and start achieving your goals.

How to mend the Leaks of Life

The "leaks" in your life drain your energy, time, and resources without providing any real benefit. Identifying and addressing these metaphorical leaks is essential for maintaining progress and resilience on life's journey. Here's how you can use the leaks concept to design your life:

- **Identify leaks of your life**: Reflect and identify the areas in your life where you feel drained, or stuck, and experiencing difficulties, setbacks, or challenges. These could be related to health, lifestyle, relationships, family issues, work, finance, spiritual, or other areas of your activities that don't align with your values or goals.

Identify Your Weaknesses	
Domains	**Personal Weaknesses** (Leaks) Name:
Physical & Behavioral	
Psychological	
Intellectual	
Spiritual	

- **Assess the impact**: Determine the severity of these leaks. Some leaks may be minor inconvenience, while other could be major problems. Evaluate how each of these leaks affecting your well-being and progress towards your goals.

- **Prioritize leaks**: Based on the severity of leaks, prioritize the urgency and prepare time bound action plan to address them.
- **Plug Immediate Leaks**: Start with the leaks that are causing the most immediate harm or disruption. These could be crises that require immediate attention, such as health issues, financial troubles, or. Take proactive steps to address these issues and prevent further damage. This could involve changing the wrong lifestyle, unhealthy diet, failing commitments, negative attitude, perfectionism, etc.
- **Adjust the Course**: Check whether you are heading towards your goals and aspirations, or drifting away from your goals. Identify and change your values, habits, routines, or long-term plans to stay on track.
- **Strengthen your Resources**: Positive psychology recommends, instead of focusing on leaks or negative aspects of your personality, strengthen your resources (body, mind, intellect, & spirit) to withstand future leaks by enhancing your physical, emotional, intellectual, and spiritual capabilities.
- **Navigate your journey**: Regularly monitor your life to ensure that old leaks (negative aspects) don't resurface and new ones don't emerge. Focus on harnessing the positive energy and momentum that comes from living more intentionally and authentically. Set sails toward your goals with renewed clarity, purpose, and enthusiasm.

By using the concept of leaks from the sailboat metaphor, you can identify and address the personal weaknesses, which are holding you back.

Personal Weaknesses & Strengths

> **Exercise:** Identify weaknesses (leaks) of your personality, which are retarding or preventing progress in your life. Assess the impact of leaks. Prioritize the leaks and make an action plan to overcome your personal weaknesses.

Step 6: Enhance Your Strengths

Develop and leverage your strengths: In the sailboat "Sails" capture the wind's power and convert it into movement, propelling the boat in the desired direction. They can be adjusted based on wind direction and strength to optimize speed and course.

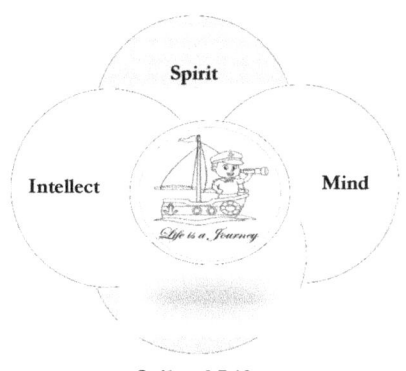

Sails of Life

Similarly, **in the life journey,** "personal strengths" are the qualities, knowledge and skills that enable us to overcome challenges, achieve goals, and live a fulfilling life. Strengths act as the driving force that helps us navigate life's currents, both calm and stormy.

A strong sailboat needs a variety of sails working together. In personal life we are equipped with four kinds of natural sails- physical, psychological, intellectual, and spiritual. By developing different strengths, we become adaptable and capable of handling various situations.

Just as a sailboat with well-maintained and adjusted sails performs better, a life guided by strong personal strengths allows you to:

- **Move forward:** Your strengths provide the motivation and determination to pursue your goals and dreams.
- **Navigate challenges:** When faced with obstacles, your strengths help you find solutions, adapt strategies, and persevere.
- **Stay on course:** Your strengths act as a compass, guiding you towards what holds meaning and value for you.

There will be times when the wind isn't favourable. Don't be discouraged. Use your personal strengths to withstand the storm and adjust your sails to find a new course. Enjoy the Journey!

So, by identifying and cultivating your personal strengths, you equip yourself with a powerful set of "sails" to navigate the vast ocean of life.

The positive psychology emphasizes the continuous enhancement of personal strengths, rather than focusing solely on weaknesses and plugging the leaks. Here is how you can enhance personal strengths of your personality;

Dysfunctional Belief

My strengths are my current talents, which are validated by my success. I don't need to learn any new skill

Reframe (Functional Belief)

I acknowledge my current strengths and the accomplishments. I will continue to develop new skills and talents seeking to learn and grow.

My Personal Strengths

Strength of Sails

Sails	Strengths Required	How to enhance?
Physical Sail	Good health, physical fitness, stamina, resilience, coordination, and enthusiasm to live an active and happy life..	Enhance physical strength through proper nutrition, exercise, rest, self-care, and a balanced lifestyle.
Psychological Sail	The mind encompasses your thoughts, beliefs, emotions, self-awareness, emotional regulation, and optimism. Mind directs your actions and decisions.	Enhance psychological strength by cultivating a positive mindset, emotional resilience, mindfulness practices, and effective mind management.
Intellectual Sail	The intellect refers to cognitive abilities, knowledge, curiosity, problem solving, and intellectual capacities. It represents your capacity for reasoning, problem-solving, creativity, and learning.	Enhance intellectual strength by goal clarity, continuous learning, critical thinking, and expanding your knowledge base.
Spiritual Sail	The spirit represents your source of divine energy, values, and connection to divine force. It encompasses your inner peace and happiness, sense of meaning, spirituality, and personal beliefs.	Enhance spiritual power by developing self-awareness, practicing gratitude, cultivating compassion and empathy. Practicing yoga and meditation.

The following table briefly describes what strengths need to be enhanced to make a successful and fulfilling life:

Enhancing the Personal Strengths		
Area	*How to improve Personal Strengths*	*Techniques*
Physical	**Self-Care and Well-Being**: take care of physical and mental well-being by maintaining a healthy lifestyle. **Self-discipline:** Follow a disciplined life in every area of activity **Stay Flexible and Adaptive**: Be open to new ideas, perspectives, and experiences. **Expand Your Network**: build a strong network that can provide guidance, encouragement, and assistance along your journey.	Lifestyle change, Exercise
Psychological	**Positive Emotions**: To propel the boat forward learn to cultivate positive emotions like gratitude, love, joy, hope, tolerance, engagement, etc. **Virtues and Character Strengths:** Develop character strengths to harness and navigate through life. **Mindfulness:** Monitor your thoughts, feelings, and experiences to tune with wind direction, currents, and changes in weather.	Positive Psychology, PERMA, Mindfulness, Building Character Strengths

Personal Weaknesses & Strengths

	Reframe dysfunctional beliefs to shift your perspectives toward positivity	
Intellectual	**Cultivate a growth mindset** to grow your strengths and embrace challenges as opportunities for growth and learning. **Goal Setting and Planning**: strengthen your sails by setting clear goals, creating action plans, and staying focused on your desired outcomes. **Continuous Learning**: continuously expand your knowledge and skills such as problem-solving and leadership skills. **Build Resilience**: Cultivate a positive mindset, learn from setbacks, and bounce back stronger when faced with challenges. Develop coping strategies to manage adverse circumstances in life. **Take Calculated Risks**: Assess risks carefully and take calculated risks that can lead to growth and new opportunities.	Growth mindset, Learning
Spiritual	**Self-Reflection**: Sailing offers moments of solitude and introspection to reflect on the journey and make adjustments as needed. **Self-awareness:** Acquire spiritual knowledge from	Spiritual Transformation, Yoga and Meditation

	realized gurus and study of scriptures. Spirit is the sentient force, source of happiness, and life energy. Spiritual awareness connects your mind with the spirit to tap divine energy and bliss.	
	Purify your mind: By spiritual awakening get rid of mental impurities like selfish desires, greed, ego, hatred, anger, delusion, jealousy, fear, etc.	
	Inner Peace: Practice yoga and meditation to attain inner peace and happiness.	

Personal strength Enhancement techniques

For the consistent forward journey of life, the personal strengths of physical, psychological, intellectual, and spiritual personalities must be continuously improved using various learning techniques. A brief introduction of some important personal strength development techniques is presented here:

- Lifestyles Change
- Positive Psychology
- Psychological Tendencies
- PERMA
- Mindfulness
- Character Strengths
- Growth Mindset
- Practical Spirituality
- Raj Yoga

1. Lifestyle Change

A lifestyle changes deals with making significant modifications to one's habits, behaviours, and choices that affect health well-being, and happiness. It often involves adapting healthier practices in areas such as diet, exercise, sleep, stress management, and social interactions. The objective of lifestyle change is to improve physical, mental, and spiritual health, enhance quality of life, and prevent chronic diseases. Lifestyle change involves the following main activities:

- **Healthy Diet:** Use more fruits, vegetables, whole grains, and lean proteins in your diet while reducing processed foods, sugars, and unhealthy fats.
- **Disciplined Routine:** Following a structured time discipline for eating, working, sleeping, exercise, meditation, relaxation, and other activities according to laws of nature.
- **Regular Exercise:** Ensuring a consistent exercise routine that includes activities like walking, running, yogic asanas, and strength training exercises to improve overall fitness.
- **Adequate Sleep:** Taking sufficient sleep each night, typically around 7-9 hours for most adults, to support physical and mental well-being.
- **Meditation:** Everyone is a spiritual being. Spirituality is not connected with any religion; it is a universal technique to connect you with your inner Self. To attain inner peace and true happiness Meditation is a well-proven technique, it must be part of daily routine.
- **Stress Management:** Practicing stress-reduction techniques such as mindfulness meditation, *pranayama*, or

engaging in hobbies and other play activities that promote relaxation.
- **No Alcohol and Tobacco:** No use of alcohol, and tobacco in any form to reduce the risk of various health problems.
- **Commitment & Practice:** Lifestyle changes require strong commitment and willpower, consistent practice, self-discipline, and perseverance, effects are well known to everyone, which will lead to a healthy body, cheerful mind, inner peace, and true happiness in life.

2. Positive Psychology

Positive psychology focuses on understanding and promoting the positive aspects of human experiences, such as happiness, well-being, resilience, and personal strengths. While traditional psychology often focuses on identifying and treating mental health problems, positive psychology seeks to enhance the quality of life and promote flourishing by studying what makes life worth living.

The fundamental approach of positive psychology is about shifting the focus from what is wrong with people to what is right with them. Instead of merely studying disorders and dysfunction, positive psychology examines the factors that contribute to a fulfilling and meaningful life. It explores basic aspects like:

- What makes people happy?
- What are the ingredients of a meaningful life?
- How can we cultivate resilience in the face of adversity?
- What are people's strengths, and how can they be used to enhance well-being?

One of the key concepts in positive psychology is subjective well-being, which refers to how people evaluate their own lives in terms of happiness and life satisfaction. Positive psychology also emphasizes the importance of personal strengths and virtues. Instead of focusing solely on weaknesses, positive psychology encourages individuals to identify and leverage their unique strengths to overcome challenges and achieve their goals. By recognizing and nurturing their strengths, people can enhance their resilience, performance, and overall well-being.

Practical applications of positive psychology include interventions and practices designed to enhance happiness and well-being, such as gratitude exercises, mindfulness meditation, acts of kindness, and strengths-based interventions.

By focusing on the positive aspects of human experience and harnessing people's strengths and virtues, positive psychology seeks to empower individuals to lead happier, more fulfilling lives.

3.Psychological Tendencies

In the sailboat metaphor, we discussed about the "leaks"- the personal weaknesses, that drain energy, and consume time and effort for patching them. According to positive psychology, instead of focusing on personal weaknesses, the focus should be shifted to enhancing the personal strengths.

In the current era of high-tech world, the life philosophy adopted by most professionals is highly influenced by five psychological tendencies: materialism, perfectionism, social comparison, maximizing, and physical inactivity.

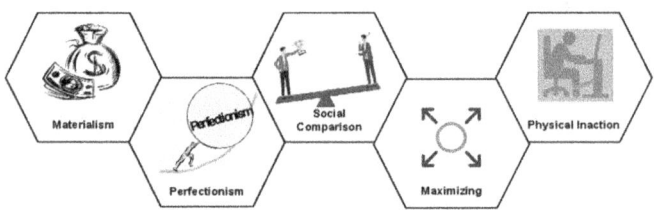

Negative Psychological Tendencies

These are observed as the personal weaknesses (leaks) and the root causes of unhappiness of the new generation, despite success in career and good wealth creation. The people affected by these weaknesses (leaks) are mostly corporate and IT professionals, who are most of the time interacting with their computers (less with human beings) resulting in various health, psychological, and behavioural problems.

- **Materialism:** the belief that money and possessions are the most important in life. For the materialist, wealth is the indicator of success or happiness, and they prioritize the pursuit of material goods and financial gain over other values such as relationships, personal development, or spirituality.

    Recommended Solutions: Shift your perspective to meaningful aspects of life. The practice of detachment, gratitude, simplicity. Developing contentment, purposeful life, meaningful relationships, service attitude. Setting meaningful goals, focus on experiences. Developing spiritual awareness, and practicing meditation.

- **Perfectionism:** the tendency to set excessively high standards for oneself and others. Striving for flawlessness, and being overly critical of one's own performance. People with perfectionistic tendencies often have a strong desire to achieve perfection in all areas of life, including work, relationships, and personal endeavours. They develop stress for themselves and others working with them.

Recommended Solutions: Set realistic goals, focus on progress rather perfection, self-compassion, embrace mistakes as opportunities, set time limits, consider failure as feedback, convert mistakes into opportunities, take professional help, practice mindfulness, meditation.

- **Social comparison** is a process through which individuals evaluate themselves by comparing their attitudes, abilities, opinions, and traits to those of others. This comparison can occur in various domains, such as intelligence, attractiveness, wealth, success, and social status. This develops inferiority or superiority complex and imbalanced behaviour with others.

    Recommended Solutions: Minimize social media use, identify triggers, focus on your strengths. Set realistic goals, believe in your uniqueness, self-compassion, improve your self-esteem, cultivate supportive relationships. Practice gratitude, mindfulness, meditation

- **Maximizing:** a psychological tendency of some people who are "maximizers", strive to get the very best out of every decision. They take a long time to make a decision and are never happy with their final choice. They do have open ended upper limit of their expectations. On the other hand, "satisficers" opt for a choice that meets their criteria, tend to adopt a "this is good enough" approach, make quick decisions, and feel happy.

    Recommended Solutions: Recognize the adverse impact of maximizing. Set realistic expectations, and your upper limit standard. Develop good decision-making skills, consider pros and cons of choices, narrow down your choices, set decision deadlines. Learn to tolerate uncertainties, Practice self-compassion, gratitude, mindfulness, meditation.

- **Physical Inactivity:** A tendency of some people, who don't want to do any physical work other than sitting at a desk or computer, lying on the sofa watching television, or engaging in activities that involve minimal physical effort. Physical inactivity is a significant public health concern with various negative consequences for both physical and mental well-being.

    Recommended Solutions: Recognize the health benefits of physical actions, enjoy actions, set your routine. Develop a "do-it-now" attitude, make a "to-do" list, don't procrastinate. Start with small goals for activities, set reminders for yourself. Develop a sense of responsibility, involve others, improve your environment, reorganize yourself. Practice regular exercise, yoga and meditation.

To attain the goals of physical, family, work, and spiritual lives, and live a meaningful life, it's important and urgent to overcome the above five personal weaknesses. It can be effectively done by adapting positive psychology and spiritual practices.

4.PERMA Model

Suffering and happiness, both are part of the human condition, and psychology should care about each. Traditionally, a major focus of psychology has been to relieve human suffering. Whereas, human strengths, excellence, and flourishing are just as authentic as human suffering. People want to cultivate the best version of themselves and live a meaningful life. They want to grow their capacities for love and compassion, creativity and curiosity, work and resilience, and integrity and wisdom. But, how to do it?

To answer these fundamental questions is PERMA:

- **Positive Emotions (P):** This aspect focuses on experiencing positive emotions such as joy, gratitude, serenity, interest, hope, pride, amusement, inspiration, and love. Cultivating positive emotions is essential for overall well-being. Within limits, we can increase our positive emotions about the past by cultivating gratitude and forgiveness. Our positive emotions about the present can be increased by enjoying physical pleasure and mindfulness. Positive emotions about the future can be increased by building hope and optimism.

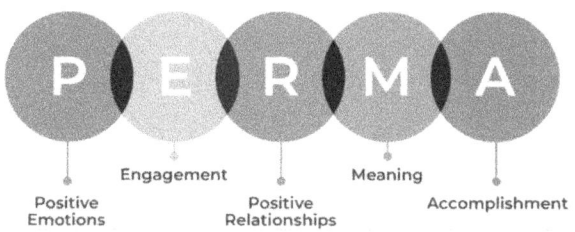

PERMA Model of Wellbeing

- **Engagement (E):** Engagement refers to the state of being fully absorbed and deeply involved in activities that are challenging and meaningful to us. Engagement is an experience in which someone fully deploys their skills, strengths, and attention for a challenging task, often losing track of time and feeling a sense of "flow" - a state of complete immersion and focus. Flow can be experienced in a wide variety of activities, e.g., a good conversation, a work task, playing a musical instrument, reading a book, writing, fixing a bike, gardening, cooking, sports performance, etc.

- **Relationships (R):** Relationships are fundamental to well-being and happiness. The experiences that contribute to happiness are often amplified through our relationships in the form of great joy, meaning, laughter, a feeling of belonging, and pride in accomplishment. Connections to others can give life purpose and meaning. Connecting with family members, friends, colleagues, and community members provides social support, fosters a sense of belonging, and enhances overall happiness and satisfaction.

- **Meaning (M):** Finding meaning and purpose in life involves identifying our core values, goals, and beliefs and aligning our actions with them. Having a sense of meaning gives us a reason to live, motivates us to pursue our goals, and provides a framework for making sense of life's challenges. There are various societal institutions that enable a sense of meaning, such as family, religion, science, politics, work organizations, justice, the community, social causes, etc. Voluntary service and association with such service organizations can make our life meaningful.

- **Accomplishment (A):** Accomplishment refers to setting and achieving goals, mastering new skills, and experiencing a sense of competence and achievement. Accomplishments can be both big and small, and they contribute to feelings of satisfaction, self-efficacy, and self-esteem. People pursue accomplishment, competence, success, and mastery for their own sake, in a variety of domains, including the work, profession, sports, games, hobbies, social service, etc.

The PERMA model suggests that well-being is not solely determined by the absence of negative experiences but, is also influenced by the presence of positive factors in our lives. By focusing on enhancing positive emotions, engagement, relationships, meaning, and accomplishment, individuals can cultivate a more fulfilling and meaningful life.

5. Mindfulness

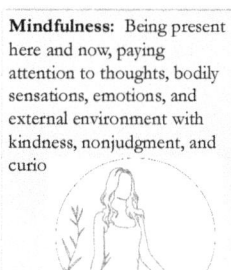

Mindfulness: Being present here and now, paying attention to thoughts, bodily sensations, emotions, and external environment with kindness, nonjudgment, and curio

Imagine you are sitting by a calm lake located in a beautiful natural environment of Himalayan mountains, watching the gentle ripples on the water surface.

Your mind is focused solely on the beauty and tranquility of this moment. You're not thinking about what happened yesterday or what might happen tomorrow. You're fully in present, embracing the sights, sounds, and sensations around you. This state of being fully attentive and engaged in the present moment, what we call mindfulness.

Mindfulness is a way of paying attention to here and now, without judgment or distraction. It's about tuning into your thoughts, feelings, bodily sensations, and surroundings with openness and curiosity. Instead of dwelling on the past or worrying about the future, mindfulness encourages you to anchor yourself in the present moment, appreciating it for what it is.

At its core, mindfulness is about awareness. It's about noticing the thoughts that pass through your mind, observing the sensations in your body, and acknowledging the emotions that arise within you. But it's not just about being aware; it's also about acceptance. Mindfulness teaches us to embrace our experiences without trying to change them or judge them as good or bad.

Popular mindfulness practices include mindfulness meditation, body scan exercises, mindful breathing, and mindful walking. During mindfulness meditation, you might focus your attention on your breath, the sensations in your body, or the sounds around you. When your mind inevitably wanders, as it naturally does, you gently bring your focus back to the present moment without self-criticism. Through regular meditation practice, you can train your mind to become more mindful in your everyday life.

Mindfulness is a way of life. It is about bringing mindfulness into your daily activities, whether you're eating, walking, doing your work, or interacting with others. It's about fully enjoying each moment, finding joy in the simple things, and being fully present in whatever you're doing. Regular practice of mindfulness can significantly improve your well-being. It can help reduce stress, anxiety, and depression, improve your focus and concentration, enhance your relationships, and increase

6. Character Strengths

People often look for good character strengths in others, whether they are family members, friends, colleagues, employees or any other person. Now, it is time to identify and enhance character strengths of your own personality.

Character strengths are positive personality traits that are personally fulfilling, morally valued and core to our being or identity. When we express our character strengths, we produce positive outcomes, boost well-being such as positive relations, and contribute to the greater collective good.

Professional success without deep fulfilment is all too common. By tuning into and using our character strengths at work and personal lives, we can increase our efficiency, engagement, wellbeing and discover more meaning and sense in our profession. If we are feeling physically, emotionally and intellectually energized but lacking in meaning and purpose, character strengths might be the missing part of our personality.

Martin Seligman, one of the founding members of positive psychology, and Neal Meyerson created the Values In-Action Institute and identified 24 good character strengths.

Building on one's positive character strengths can help people develop skills to face the challenges of life and improve emotional wellbeing. The 24-character strengths are divided into six classes of virtues (goodness): wisdom, courage, humanity, justice, temperance, and transcendence, which are briefly described in the following table:

Positive Character Strengths

Virtues (Goodness)	24 Character Strengths
Wisdom: Wisdom includes the character strengths that lead people to acquire knowledge and use it in creative and useful ways.	• **Creativity**: Thinking of new ways to do things • **Curiosity**: Taking an interest in a wide variety of topics • **Open-mindedness**: Examining things from all sides; thinking things through • **Love of learning**: Mastering new topics, skills, and bodies of research • **Perspective**: Being able to provide wise counsel to others; looking at the world in a way that makes sense
Courage: Courage has emotional character strengths that allow people to accomplish goals despite any opposition they face.	• **Honesty**: Speaking the truth; being authentic and genuine • **Bravery**: Embracing challenges, difficulties, or pain; not shrinking from threat • **Persistence**: Finishing things once they are started • **Zest**: Approaching all things in life with energy and excitement
Humanity: A range of interpersonal character strengths that involve caring for and befriending others.	• **Kindness**: Doing Favors and good deeds • **Love**: Valuing close relations with others • **Social Intelligence:** Being aware of other people's motives and feelings
Justice: People who are strong in justice tend to possess civic strengths that underscore the importance of a healthy community.	• **Fairness**: Treating all people the same • **Leadership**: Organizing group activities and making sure they happen • **Teamwork**: Working with others as a group or a team

Temperance: Temperance tends to have strengths that protect against the excesses in life.	<ul><li>**Forgiveness**: Forgiving others who have wronged them</li><li>**Modesty**: Letting one's successes and accomplishments stand on their own</li><li>**Prudence**: Avoiding doing things they might regret; **making good choices**</li><li>**Self-regulation**: Being disciplined; controlling one's appetites and emotions</li></ul>
Transcendence: Transcendence tends to forge connections with the Soul, the universe, or God that provide meaning, purpose, and understanding.	<ul><li>**Appreciation of beauty**: Noticing and appreciating beauty and excellence in everything</li><li>**Gratitude**: Being thankful for the good things; taking time to express thanks</li><li>**Hope**: Expecting the best; working to make it happen; believing good things are possible</li><li>**Humour**: Making other people smile or laugh; **enjoying jokes**</li><li>**Religiousness:** Having a solid belief about a higher purpose and meaning of life</li></ul>

Developing and internalizing character strengths involve cultivating positive traits, attitudes, and behaviours that contribute to overall well-being and success. People who express their character strengths tend to be less stressed, more engaged, energized, and happier.

7. Growth Mindset

Stanford University psychologist Carol Dweck found in her research that the personality of individuals is driven by the basic belief of a "fixed mindset" or "growth mindset". A fixed mindset is a belief that abilities and intelligence are static

Growth Mindset

Fixed Mindset

traits that cannot be significantly changed. A growth mindset, on the other hand, is a belief or attitude that individuals can develop their abilities and intelligence through dedication, effort, and learning. For a successful life journey, individuals can improve their personality and competence by developing a growth mindset. Key characteristics of a growth mindset include:

- **Embracing Challenges:** A growth mindset makes individuals embrace challenges as opportunities for growth and learning, instead of avoiding them as difficulties.
- **Valuing Effort:** People with a growth mindset recognize the importance of effort and hard work in achieving success. They continue to invest adequate time and effort to achieve their goals.
- **Perseverance:** Persistence in doing something despite difficulty or delay in achieving success. Failures or setbacks cannot discourage a person with a growth mindset. They take it as a challenge and opportunity to prove their competence.
- **Take Feedback:** Individuals with a growth mindset actively seek feedback and constructive criticism from the concerned people to help them improve. They see feedback as valuable input for learning and growth.
- **Inspired by Others' Success:** Individuals with a growth mindset learn from successful people and competitors. They see others' achievements as evidence

of what is possible and use them as motivation to strive for their own goals.

- **Positive attitude for Learning:** People with a growth mindset believe that their abilities and intelligence can be developed over time through learning and practice. They are always eager to acquire new knowledge and skills.

Cultivating a growth mindset can lead to greater resilience, motivation, and achievement. By embracing challenges, persisting in the face of setbacks, valuing effort, seeking feedback, being inspired by others' success, and believing in a positive attitude and learning, individuals can discover their full potential and achieve greater success in all areas of life.

8. Practical Spirituality

According to Holy *Vedas*- the ancient *Hindu* scripture, the purpose of life is to seek happiness. Everyone is striving to attain happiness (*Anand*) only, but due to ignorance and false notions searching for it in money and materialistic things, like looking for sweetness in chili. Even after attaining materialistic success in life, many ultrarich, powerful, and famous people are having no inner peace. Practical spirituality provides a validated approach to liberation from suffering and attaining inner peace and bliss.

Root causes of sufferings: According to spiritual principles, people suffer in life due to five afflictions; *avidya, asmita, raga, dvesha,* and *abhinivesha*. These are identified as the root causes of suffering, resulting in personal weaknesses (leaks) and working as the obstacles to happiness (wellbeing) in life. Unless these five causes addressed, you cannot attain true happiness in life. In fact, practical spirituality begins with addressing and elimination of the five root-causes.

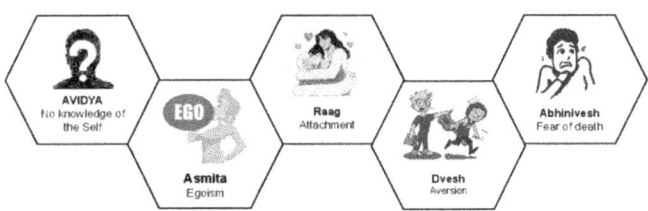

Root-Causes of Suffering

Practical spirituality is the science of life-based on the laws of nature. By learning and practicing spiritual principles, yoga, and meditation in everyday life, one can attain true and lasting inner peace, and happiness (bliss). By practicing spiritual principles, one can eliminate the following five root causes of suffering to attain true happiness and wellbeing:

Avidya **(Ignorance)**: Avidya refers to a lack of true knowledge or ignorance of the Self (Soul or Spirit). The real source of happiness and cause of existence is the Self. Because of spiritual ignorance, people mistake happiness in inert materialistic things and money resulting in suffering. Due to avidya, other afflictions; egoism, attachment, aversion, and fear arise.

Asmita **(Egoism)**: Wrong notion of oneself as "I am the doer" the sense of individuality is Ego. For example; if the universe is a grand ocean, we are with the ocean, not individual drops in the ocean. When we think as individuals drop, then we separate ourselves from the universe, this feeling is ego. This sense of separateness gives rise to feelings of pride, superiority, inferiority, and the desire for recognition. The ego propels us to selfish desires and actions.

Raga **(Attachment)**: Raga refers to longing and attachments to sensory objects and affections. Clinging to materialistic things brings temporary satisfaction, such as sensory pleasures, temporary relationships, wealth, and status.

Attachment leads to suffering when these objects of desire due to their impermanent nature fail to fulfill our expectations.

Dvesha **(Aversion)**: Dvesha is aversion or avoidance of persons, objects, and situations that cause discomfort, pain, or dissatisfaction, but it ultimately perpetuates suffering by creating resistance, inner conflict, and negative emotions.

Abhinivesha **(Fear of Death)**: Abhinivesha is the fear of death or clinging to life, the physical body, and other objects. The fear of death or losing objects leads to anxiety, attachment, and resistance to change, ultimately hindering spiritual growth and liberation.

Through learning, reflection, and practices of spiritual principles, such as the study of Upanishads, and practice of Yoga, and Meditation under guidance of realized Guru, one can gradually transcend these afflictions and experience the eternal nature of the Self; existence – knowledge - bliss (*Sat-Chit-Anand*).

9.Raj Yoga

Patanjali Yoga Sutras is a comprehensive guide to the Operating Procedure of life, based on the laws of nature, prepared by realized seers.

Patanjali Yoga is known as Raj Yoga, which translates to "Eight-Limbed Yoga" or *Astang Yoga*. The practice of eight limbs help to unite the behavioral, physical, and mental aspects of human personality with the spiritual Self to realize the true nature of the soul- *Sat-Chit-Anand*, which is the ultimate purpose of life. The eight limbs of Patanjali Yoga are briefly described here;

1. *Yama* **(Ethical Restraints)**: These are moral principles that guide one's behavior towards other beings and the world. The five behavioral conducts are Ahimsa (non-violence), Satya (truthfulness), Asteya (non-stealing), Brahmacharya (celibacy or moderation), and Aparigraha (non-possessiveness).

2. **Niyama (Observances)**: Niyama are personal practices that cultivate self-discipline and inner observance. The five rules are Saucha (cleanliness), Santosha (contentment), Tapas (self-discipline), Swadhyaya (self-study), and Ishvara Pranidhana (surrender to cosmic power).

3. **Asana (Postures)**: Asanas refer to physical postures practiced in yoga. The purpose of asanas is to prepare and maintain the body physically fit and capable of performing meditation and spiritual practice.

4. **Pranayama (Breath Control)**: Pranayama involves quietening the mind by breath control techniques that regulate the flow of prana (life force energy) in the body. Control of the mind is essential for meditation.

5. **Pratyahara (Sense Withdrawal)**: Pratyahara is the withdrawal of the senses from external stimuli and turning inward. By quieting the senses, one can cultivate greater focus and concentration, preparing the mind for meditation.

6. **Dharana (Concentration)**: Dharana is the practice of single-pointed concentration, where the mind is focused on a single object or point of awareness. Through dharana, one learns to still the fluctuations of the mind and cultivate inner steadiness.

7. **Dhyana (Meditation)**: Dhyana is the uninterrupted flow of awareness towards the object of meditation. It is a state of deep absorption and inner tranquility where the meditator experiences a sense of oneness with the object of meditation.

8. **Samadhi (Union)**: Samadhi is the ultimate goal of yoga, where the practitioner experiences a state of profound spiritual absorption and union with the Divine Self. It is a state of pure consciousness beyond individual identity, where the practitioner realizes the true nature of the Self.

By gaining spiritual knowledge and practicing yoga and meditation, spiritual transformation happens, which changes the thinking, feeling, and behavior of the practitioner from materialism to spirituality. The spiritual transformation develops virtuous qualities such as gratitude, compassion, detachment, contentment, kindness, love, fearlessness, integrity, truthfulness, etc. leading to well-being and happiness in life.

Exercise: Identify the specific physical, psychological, intellectual and spiritual strengths you want to develop to attain life goals.

***

Chapter 9
Challenges & Staying Aligned

In the journey of life, encountering challenges is inevitable. This phase focuses on developing the resilience and determination to overcome obstacles while maintaining focus on your goals and aspirations.

Challenges are inevitable part of life journey, which mut be resolved timely. Resolving challenges involves confronting obstacles head-on with problem-solving skills and resilience. It's about adopting a proactive approach to address difficulties, whether they arise from external circumstances or internal struggles. By cultivating resilience and determination, you build the strength and perseverance needed to navigate through adversity and emerge stronger on the other side.

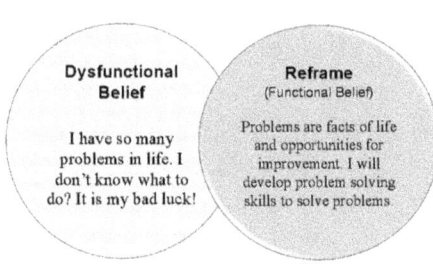

Problems in Life

Staying Aligned emphasizes the importance of maintaining alignment with your goals and values amidst life's distractions and temptations. It involves setting clear objectives, creating action plans, and regularly monitoring your progress to ensure that you're moving in the right direction. By staying focused on your goals and remaining true to your values, you avoid getting derailed by obstacles or distractions and stay committed to your journey of growth and self-discovery.

Together, resolving challenges and staying on track creates a framework for success in overcoming obstacles and achieving your aspirations. By developing resilience in the face of adversity and maintaining focus on your goals, you empower yourself to overcome challenges and stay on course towards realizing your dreams.

- Step 7: Resolve Challenges (Repairs): Tackle life's hurdles head-on through problem-solving and resilience.

- Step 8: Stay Aligned (Compass): Continuously monitor your journey, ensuring alignment with your values and goals

Step 7: Resolve Challenges

Tackle life's hurdles head-on through problem-solving and resilience: Resolve challenges is like repair of the sailboat. Throughout your life's journey, you'll encounter a variety of problems – big and small, personal and professional. During goal setting also, the gaps between the target and present state are identified as problems, which must be solved to attain the goals.

Problem-solving is one of the most desirable skills to keep your life journey on track. It's your ability to navigate the challenges, the rough seas, and unexpected conditions, and find solutions that propel you forward. It's not about avoiding problems, but rather developing the skills and mindset to tackle them effectively.

By combining "Reframing" and "design thinking" tools, you can effectively "Resolve Challenges" and navigate the obstacles that life throws your way. This approach will equip you with a more positive outlook, enable you to identify workable solutions, and ultimately steer your life towards your goals. The relevant basic concepts are briefly explained here, with some case studies;

Reframing: Seeing it differently

Reframing is a psychological technique used to change the way individuals perceive a situation or problem. It involves looking at things from a different perspective or interpreting them in a different light. Rather than seeing a situation negatively, reframing encourages individuals to find positive aspects or alternative explanations.

By challenging your assumptions and beliefs about what is possible, you can open yourself up to new opportunities and creative solutions. This shift in perspective can help people feel more resilient and motivated to overcome challenges.

An ineffective perspective is called as dysfunctional belief, which is reframed to a functional belief. For example, many senior people have a dysfunctional belief: *"I am too old to pursue my dreams."*

Perspective is totally changed by reframing: "It's never too late to pursue my passions and aspirations. Age is not a limitation but an opportunity to bring unique perspectives and experiences to

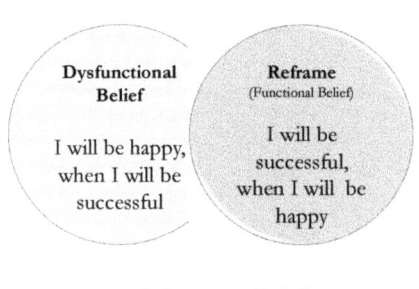

Reframe your Belief

my endeavors. I embrace every stage of life with enthusiasm and purpose."

How to apply Reframing:

- **Shift the Lens:** Don't jump to solutions. Instead, reframe the problem itself. Ask "what if" questions and consider alternative viewpoints. Is it a lack of time, or a scheduling inefficiency? Is the messy desk a sign of disorganization, or a reflection of a creative brainstorming?

- **Positive Spin:** Reframe negative situations into opportunities. A long commute can be a chance to listen to audiobooks or catch up on podcasts. A tight deadline can force you to prioritize and become more efficient.

- **Focus on Needs:** Instead of problems, consider underlying needs. Is the constant checking of your phone due to social anxiety, or a fear of missing out? By understanding the core need, you can address it directly

Reframing can be useful in situations where you feel stuck, overwhelmed, or negatively impacted by certain events or circumstances. By reframing, you can challenge limiting or dysfunctional beliefs, assumptions, or interpretations by shifting the perspective with more positive, empowering and realistic beliefs.

Reframing is a powerful tool used in design thinking and life design to shift perspectives and find new solutions to challenges. Typically, this is used to shift the perspective from Problem to Opportunity, Failure to Feedback, Constraints to Creativity, Fear to Excitement, Fixed Mindset to Growth Mindset, Isolation to Connection, Busyness to Prioritization, Comparison to Inspiration, Expectations to

Exploration, and Obstacles to Stepping Stones. Some examples of reframing are presented below:

Reframing Examples	
Dysfunctional Belief	*Reframe*
"I'm not good enough."	"I am worthy of love, success, and happiness just as I am. I acknowledge my strengths and embrace opportunities for growth."
"I'll never be able to change."	"Change is possible, and I have the power to shape my own destiny. Every small step I take towards my goals brings me closer to the person I want to become."
"I always fail at everything I try."	"Failure is a natural part of the learning process. Each setback teaches me valuable lessons and strengthens my resilience. I am capable of success with persistence and determination."
"I must always please others to be accepted."	"My worth is not dependent on others' approval. I prioritize my own needs and values while maintaining healthy relationships. Authenticity and self-respect are more important than seeking constant validation."
"I can't handle rejection or criticism."	"Rejection and criticism are opportunities for growth and self-improvement. I view feedback as constructive guidance that helps me refine my skills and approach. I am resilient and capable of overcoming challenges."
"I will never be happy until I achieve my pre-set goal."	"Happiness is a journey, not a destination. I find joy in the present moment and appreciate the progress I've made. While I work towards my goals, I cultivate gratitude and contentment in the here and now."
"I must always be in control to feel safe."	Reframe: "I acknowledge that uncertainty is a natural part of life. I trust in my ability to adapt and navigate challenges as they arise. I find strength in surrendering control and embracing the unknown with courage and resilience."
"I'll never be successful because	"My past does not define my future. I learn from my mistakes and use them as stepping stones towards success. Each day is a new

of my past mistakes."	opportunity to make positive choices and create the life I desire."
"I'm too busy to prioritize self-care and personal growth."	"Self-care and personal growth are essential for my well-being and fulfilment. I make time for activities that nourish my body, mind, and spirit, knowing that investing in myself ultimately benefits all aspects of my life."

Ultimately, reframing allows individuals to see possibilities and opportunities where they once saw only obstacles or limitations, empowering them to navigate life's challenges with greater resilience positivity, and optimism.

Design Thinking

Design thinking is a human-centred, creative problem-solving process. It is often used in the design of products, services, or experiences, now being used in "design your life" to solve problems of personal life and find new and creative solutions.

At its core, design thinking encourages individuals to approach challenges with a human-centred mindset, focusing on understanding the needs and desires of oneself and others to create innovative solutions. Design thinking process involves five steps; empathise, define, ideate, prototype and test to develop practical and innovative solutions.

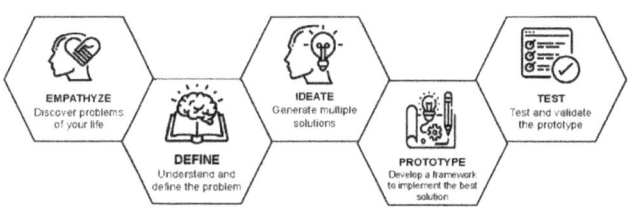

Design Thinking Process

In context of personal development, design thinking can be a transformative tool for crafting a fulfilling and meaningful life. Here is how the five steps work:

1. **Empathy:** Design thinking begins with empathy; understanding the experiences, aspirations, and challenges of oneself. By empathizing with your own desires, values, and goals of your life, you can gain insights into what truly matters to you.

2. **Define:** With a deeper understanding of yourself, you can define your goals and aspirations more clearly. What do you want to achieve? What brings you joy and fulfilment? Identify and define the problems that is stopping you to achieve your goal.

3. **Ideate:** Embrace creativity to generate a wide range of ideas for how to achieve your goals and address the problems. Brainstorm without judgment, explore unconventional possibilities, and consider multiple possible solutions to your problem.

4. **Prototype:** Select the best solution out of multiple ideas you have developed. Test out your selected ideas in small, manageable ways, develop a model for implementation.

5. **Test:** Test the implementation model (prototype). Experiment with different approaches to see what works best for you. Prototyping allows you to learn from failures and refine your strategies. Continuously refine and improve your life design based on feedback and reflection. Validate the prototype which serves your purpose or solves the problem. After validation, implement the new idea in your life to achieve the goals.

By applying the principles of design thinking to your life, you can cultivate resilience, creativity, and adaptability by solving problems of your physical, family, work, and spiritual lives

Reframing & Design Thinking

Reframing and design thinking can be combined to tackle real-life problems. Example: Imagine you're constantly flooded by emails. How to reframe and solve this problem by design thinking:

Reframing: Maybe this problem is not about the number of emails, but the inefficient way you manage them.

Design thinking:

- **Empathize:** Talk to colleagues. What are their email pain points?
- **Define:** The problem is information overload, not just email volume.
- **Ideate:** Brainstorm solutions – batch checking emails, using folders/labels, or a communication tool that integrates with email.
- **Prototype:** Implement a new system on a trial basis.
- **Test & Refine:** See if it reduces overwhelm. If not, reframe and try a different approach.

By combining reframing and design thinking, you can approach real-life problems with fresh eyes, leading to more creative and user-centered solutions.

Let us see few real-life problem-solving case studies using design thinking;

Venkat: Health Issues

Venkat is a senior management professional working in a  multinational corporation. He attended a training workshop on "Design Your Life" (DYL) and learned to use a design thinking framework to identify and solve his health problems, which are adversely impacting his professional performance, physical fitness and holistic wellbeing.

To apply design thinking, as the first step, Venkat did a self-assessment of his current state of health and evaluated a rating of 50% of his desired health norms. Based on health history, Venkat identified four main health problems; diabetes, 20% overweight, high blood pressure, and frequent headaches due to stress. Because of these issues, he has to take frequent medical leave. After the current state health evaluation, he has set a goal to improve his health to 80% level during next twelve months. Applying the positive psychology, practical spirituality, and design thinking techniques, how Venkat should solve his health problems.

Here's how Venkat could solve his health problems using the techniques of Positive Psychology, Practical Spirituality, and design thinking:

Positive Psychology: As per medical sciences, current lifestyle is resulting to psycho-somatic disease. These are due to way of thinking, feeling, and behavior of Venkat or similar people. From psychological aspects, Venkat is recommended to following activities to improve his health:

- **Focus on Strengths:** Venkat can identify his strengths related to health, such as past successes in overcoming challenges or maintaining healthy habits. This can boost his confidence and motivation.

- **Set SMART Goals:** Specific, Measurable, Achievable, Relevant, and Time-bound. Instead of just aiming to improve his health, Venkat could set smaller, more achievable goals, such as losing 5% of his body weight or reducing his headaches to once a month.

- **Practice Gratitude:** Focusing on the positive aspects of his health, like his ability to perform daily activities, can improve Venkat's overall well-being.

Practical Spirituality: Health problems are related to psychological and spiritual activities of personality. In fact, spirituality is ultimate solution for psychological, intellectual, and physical problems. Once some body learns and practice spirituality, he or she experiences positive emotions, clarity of knowledge, that improves the behavior of person, ultimately improve overall personality, including health.

- **Mind-Body Connection:** Practices like meditation or yoga can help Venkat manage stress, which is a contributing factor to his headaches.

- **Mindfulness:** Paying attention to his body's signals can help Venkat make better choices about food, exercise, and sleep. Learn mindfulness meditation from experts.

- **Purpose:** He should join a spiritual organization to learn and practice yoga and meditation to attain inner peace. Connecting to a larger purpose (beyond health) can give Venkat the motivation to stick with his spiritual and other practices.

Design Thinking: Design thinking process involves five steps; empathize, define, ideate, prototype and test to develop practical and innovative solutions. The design thinking process typically begins with a problem that needs to be solved. The first step is to understand and discover the problem, followed by the second step to define it as clearly as possible. Once the problem is defined, the next step is to generate multiple ideas of possible solutions. The ideation is done through brainstorming and other creative thinking techniques. After a list of potential solutions is generated, the fourth step is to select the best solution and develop a prototype (model) for the fifth step of testing. Once the prototype is tested and validated, it is implemented at full scale and in this way the problem is solved. Venkat is recommended to solve his health problems using the following five-phase strategy;

- **Empathize:** Venkat can consider how his health problems are affecting different areas of his life. This can help him stay motivated to make changes.

- **Define:** Clearly define the problem. Instead of just saying he wants to improve his health, Venkat could identify specific areas he wants to focus on, such as weight loss, blood pressure management, or stress reduction. Consult medical experts and undergo comprehensive health check-up.

- **Ideate:** Brainstorm a variety of solutions for each problem. For example, to lose weight, Venkat could consider different diet plans or exercise programs.

Consult dietician, yoga trainers and concerned specialists.

- **Prototype:** Test out a few of his ideas on a small scale. This will help Venkat see what works for him and what doesn't. Try various options of diet, exercise, lifestyle changes.

- **Test:** Track his progress and make adjustments to his plan as needed. Select the most effective option to make it as regular practice.

By combining these techniques, Venkat can develop a comprehensive plan to improve his health and well-being. It's important to note that this is just a general overview, and Venkat may need to tailor these techniques to his specific needs and circumstances.

Sony: A Maximiser

Sony, an IT professional, employed in a reputed global IT company. Her spouse also works in a leading corporate organization. She is living in a luxurious apartment with two school-going children and her husband. She is earning a very good salary, is a maximiser by attitude, and is always in search of a better job with a higher salary package. Despite a good income and high-profile job, she compares herself with other IT professionals and wants to be always better than others. She is a perfectionist in nature at home and at the workplace, uncertain about the future with fear of losing her job due to ongoing layoffs. Even after all her materialistic achievements, she is stressed, does not have inner peace, feels an emptiness in life, and remains unhappy.

Sony contacted a "Design Your Life" coach to find out solutions to how she can attain happiness by changing her attitude, drive out fear, identify and solve her life problems, and attain inner peace by practicing spirituality? She wants to adapt "design your life" framework to overcome the current problems of her life.

Sony's situation calls for a comprehensive approach to address her challenges and cultivate happiness. DYL coach recommended the following solutions to Sony;

Attitude Change *by Positive Psychology*

- **Gratitude Practice:** Practicing gratitude is a powerful way to cultivate happiness and well-being. To practice gratitude Sony is advised to keep a gratitude journal, noting down three things she's grateful for each day, this can shift her focus from comparison to appreciation. Some other practical ways to incorporate gratitude into daily routine include; expressing gratitude to others, reflect on past blessings, practice mindfulness meditation, count blessings before bed, and use visual reminders. By integrating these practices into daily life, Sony can cultivate a habit of gratitude that contributes to greater happiness, resilience, and overall well-being.

- **Strength Focus:** Sony should identify her strengths and achievements, focus on her own progress rather than comparing herself to others. This will boost her self-esteem and reduce stress.
- **Driving out fear:** To overcome fear related to uncertainties in life, Sony requires a combination of mindset change, practical strategies, coping mechanisms, and spiritual awareness. To tackle the fear; focus on what you can control, develop a financial security fund, and practice mindfulness and acceptance. Challenge negative thoughts, seek support of family members and friends. Focus on personal growth, create a contingency plan. By implementing these strategies Sony can gradually reduce her fear of job loss and uncertainties in life, allowing her to approach challenges with resilience, optimism, and confidence
- **Positive Affirmations:** Sony can use positive affirmations to challenge negative thoughts and build a more optimistic mindset. For example, she can repeat affirmations like "I am capable and resilient" or "I trust in my ability to navigate challenges."

Problem Solving *by Design Thinking*

- **Problem Identification:** Sony should use design thinking to analyze her fears and uncertainties about the future. By breaking down her concerns into manageable chunks, she can develop strategies to address them.
- **Ideation and Prototyping:** Sony can brainstorm potential solutions to her job insecurity, such as updating her skills, networking, or exploring

alternative career paths. She should test these ideas and iterate based on feedback.
- **Human-Cantered Design:** Sony should consider the needs and desires of her family when designing her life. Open communication and collaboration with her spouse and children can lead to solutions that benefit everyone.

Inner Peace *by Spirituality*

- **Mindfulness Practice:** Sony can practice mindfulness meditation to quiet her mind and cultivate a sense of inner peace. Daily mindfulness sessions, even just a few minutes long, can help her manage stress and anxiety.
- **Acceptance of Inevitable:** Sony should recognize that some things are beyond her control, such as layoffs in her company. By accepting this uncertainty and focusing on what she can control, she can reduce her anxiety and find peace.
- **Being Spiritual:** Sony can explore spiritual practices that resonate with her beliefs, whether it is prayer, meditation, joining a spiritual mission, or connecting with nature. These practices can provide comfort and a sense of purpose.

Design Your Life

- **Values Clarification:** Sony should reflect on her core values and priorities in life. By aligning her actions with these values, she can create a more meaningful and fulfilling life.
- **Work-Life Balance:** Sony should strive for a healthy balance between her career and personal life.

This may involve setting boundaries, delegating tasks, and prioritizing self-care.

- **Seeking Support:** Sony should not hesitate to seek support from friends, family, or a therapist if she's struggling with her mental health. A support network can provide encouragement, guidance, and perspective.

By integrating the above approaches, Sony can design a life that is characterized by fulfilment, resilience, and inner peace. She can cultivate happiness by shifting her mindset, addressing her fears with creativity and courage, and connecting with her deeper sense of purpose and spirituality.

Romesh: Stuck in Life

Romesh, a marketing professional started his career in a multinational auto component company as a sales executive. But due to his inflexible behavior and disciplined culture of the company he could not adjust with the work environment. He was looking for other alternative job, where he can experience more freedom in his workstyle. After few years, he got an opportunity as a sales manager in a medium scale private sector enterprise dealing with similar products. He was performing well and happy for some time, but due to his behavioural inflexibility he started to experience discomfort again. To realize his high ambition, and autocratic behaviour, in association with couple of friends, he made a plan to start up their own enterprise. Finally, they started a company to make some auto components in their own brand and started marketing. But this venture also could not succeed, due to poor brand competitiveness and financial constraints. Accepting the reality, his friends took up jobs in other companies, but Romesh continued to do marketing of products in his own brand, which were manufactured by some small-scale industries. Due to increasing family needs, and maintaining his

unique lifestyle, now he feels his income is not sufficient. Romesh started to explore other alternatives in the same field. Incidentally, he got an opportunity to join as marketing head of a medium scale, traditionally family-owned auto component manufacturing company. But again, his inflexibility and autocracy became the barrier to adjust with younger owners of the company. Now he is stuck in life.

How to get unstuck: Romesh can get unstuck in his life, by using design thinking, positive psychology, and practical spirituality concepts of "Design Your Life" in the following ways:

Design Thinking: Romesh can apply design thinking to solve his problem in the following ways:

- **Empathize:** Romesh can start by taking a step back and reflecting on his values, needs, and interests. What kind of work environment does he thrive in? What are his long-term career goals? Once he has a better understanding of himself, he can start to look for opportunities that are a good fit.

- **Define the Problem:** Romesh's problem is that he keeps finding himself in jobs that are a bad fit for him. This is often because he is not taking the time to carefully consider his options before making a decision.

- **Ideate:** Brainstorm a variety of different work options that could be a good fit for Romesh. This could include traditional jobs, freelance work, or starting his own business.

- **Prototype:** Once Romesh has a few ideas, he can start to experiment with them. This could involve talking to people in different fields, taking online courses, or volunteering.

- **Test:** As Romesh experiments with different options, he can start to see which ones are a good fit for him. He can then make a decision about which path to pursue.

Positive Psychology: Positive psychology can help Romesh to change is attitude in following ways:

- **Strengths:** Romesh can benefit from focusing on his strengths. The case study mentions that he was performing well as a sales manager. What skills and qualities helped him to be successful in that role? How can he leverage those strengths in his current situation? He should focus on improving his behavioral qualities, especially to increase flexibility in his approach, and respecting other's views also.

- **Weaknesses:** Romesh's main weaknesses are his inflexible behaviour and autocratic way of working. Emphasis on his own views and approach and no consideration of suggestion of others, especially owners and seniors of the employer organizations. To overcome this attitude, he needs to consult professional counsellor, to identify and change his values.

- **Gratitude:** Romesh can also practice gratitude. Taking the time to appreciate the good things in his life can help him to feel more positive and optimistic. He should be grateful to his family, employer organizations, colleagues and seniors to support him to reach this stage. This can help him to approach his job search with a humbler attitude.

Practical Spirituality: Real solutions of life problems can come from spirituality only. Every problem is temporary *"even this will pass away"* is the great spiritual principle, which can help Romesh to face the problem and find right solution in life.

- **Purpose:** Romesh can also benefit from thinking about his purpose in life. What does he want to achieve with his career? What kind of impact does he want to make on the world? Having a sense of purpose can give Romesh a sense of direction and motivation.

- **Meditation:** Romesh can join a spiritual organization to gain true knowledge to develop spiritual awareness and practice Meditation and Mindfulness. Mindfulness is the practice of paying attention to the present moment without judgment. This can help Romesh to become more aware of his thoughts and feelings, and to respond to them in a healthy way. Meditation can bring contentment, humbleness, acceptance and inner peace.

In addition to above solutions, Ramesh should take help of a mentor, who can provide guidance and support as he navigates his career. He should network with professionals, who can help Romesh to learn about new opportunities and make connections with people who can help him advance his career. Romesh should enhance his knowledge and skills relevant to his area of work. There are a variety of courses and training programs available that can help Romesh to develop new skills and learn more about different career paths.

By using a combination of design thinking, positive psychology, and practical spirituality, Romesh can develop a more fulfilling career path.

> **Exercise:** Identify problems of your life. Make a list and prioritize according to importance and urgency. Solve the problems according to priority.

Step 8: Stay Aligned

The "compass" in the sailboat metaphor represents the "inner guidance system" that individuals rely on to navigate the journey of life with clarity, purpose, and integrity. By staying true to their values, and life view, individuals can chart a path toward their desired destination (goals) with confidence and determination.

Compass of Life

The compass of your life can give you feedback, whether you are heading towards right direction.

It works as emotional barometer, if you are on the right path compass will reflect your wellbeing. Conversely, if you feel any discomfort, it warns you to retrospect and take course correction.

Direction of life: In real life situation, every facet of your life is under control of the mind. It operates like a compass used by the captain of the sailboat, which is providing insights into

Design Your Life

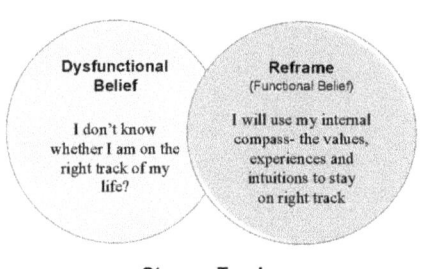

Stay on Track

the direction and course of life's journey relative to goals, aspirations and destinations. Your ultimate life objective (happiness) and personal values serve as the true north, and mind acting as the needle or indicator of the compass. The mind continuously evaluates the external environment and internal states much like a compass, it assesses the direction of life journey, emotions, thoughts and providing feedback. When you feel contented, fulfilled, and in harmony with your values, it serves as positive feedback, indicating that you are on the right path. Conversely, feelings of discomfort, guilt, or conflict may signal that you are deviating from your values, prompting you to reassess your choices.

Intuitive guidance: In addition to rational analysis, the mind offers intuitive guidance, as subtle feedback based on your instincts and subconscious perceptions. Gut feelings, instincts, and subconscious signals provide valuable insights and direction, especially in complex or ambiguous situations, alerting you to potential opportunities or warning signs that may not be immediately perceivable.

Destination: Just as a sailor uses a compass to track progress towards destination, your inner compass helps you evaluate whether you are moving closer to your goals of life. Attaining milestones (means goals) of your journey on physical, family, work and spiritual pathways, overcoming challenges, and witnessing personal growth serve as positive feedback, reaffirming that you are making meaningful progress. On the other hand, stagnation or setbacks may signal the need for adjustments or renewed focus. When deviations occur from the intended path, whether due to external influences or internal conflicts, the mind facilitates course corrections. It learns from past experiences, adapts to changing circumstances, and adjusts behaviors to realign with goals and values.

By cultivating awareness of your inner compass and actively seeking feedback from your experiences, emotions, and intuition, you can navigate life's journey with greater confidence, resilience, and alignment with your values and goals.

> **Exercise:** Reflect on your life journey progressing on physical, family, work, and spiritual pathways. Use your mental compass to assess the current direction of your life: are you experiencing positive emotions (happy) or negative emotions of disappointment? Develop your course correction strategy.

Chapter 10
Weathers & People Around

During the life everyone faces changing weather, which may be stormy or unpleasant, calm, cool or pleasant. At the same time, in your journey you are not alone, but surrounded by many people. Navigating life's storms and building connections with people around you are crucial aspects of the journey toward a fulfilling and meaningful life. This phase is characterized by resilience in the face of adversity and the cultivation of relationships that provide support, growth, and companionship.

Navigating Weathers involves developing the inner strength and adaptability to face life's inevitable challenges and setbacks. It's about, facing adversity with courage, perseverance, and a positive mindset, knowing that difficult times are opportunities for growth and learning. Whether it's personal setbacks, unexpected obstacles, or external crises, this step equips you with the tools and mindset to navigate turbulent times with grace and resilience.

Cultivating Relationships emphasizes the importance of fostering meaningful relationships with others around you. These connections serve as sources of support, encouragement, and inspiration throughout life's journey. By nurturing genuine and authentic relationships with family, friends, mentors, and colleagues, you create a network of support that enriches your life and provides companionship along the way. These connections offer opportunities for collaboration, mutual growth, and shared experiences, adding depth and richness to your journey.

Together, navigating storms and cultivating relationships create a sturdy foundation for a fulfilling and resilient life. By developing resilience in the face of adversity and cultivating meaningful relations with others, you empower yourself to navigate life's challenges with strength, grace, and the support of a caring community.

Step 09: Navigate Weathers (Weather): Adapt and persevere through life's unpredictable challenges and setbacks.

Step 10: Cultivate Relationships (Other Boats): Foster meaningful connections with those around you to enrich your journey

Step 9: Navigate Weathers

Adapt and persevere through life's unpredictable challenges and setbacks: In the sailboat metaphor, the "weather" represents the "external circumstances" or conditions that influence the sailboat journey. Just as a sailor cannot control the weather (wind, waves, or storms), similarly there are some events or conditions of life which are beyond your control. The three main uncontrollable aspects of the weather are explained below;

Uncontrollable Elements of Weather		
Weather	*Sailboat Journey*	*Life Journey*
Wind	The intensity and direction of the wind can push the sailboat in wrong direction- favourable or unfavourable.	Economic changes, societal trends, opportunities, challenges, relationships, and events beyond your control. Actions of others can push life in different direction.

Waves	Waves can make the sailboat float up and down exposing it to unexpected challenges in turbulent sea.	Ups and downs of life, pleasant and unpleasant events, setbacks, and moments of joy.
Storms	Storms are the crises and hardships encountered along the journey.	Loss of loved ones, breakups, serious health issues, losing job, financial problems, setbacks, disappointments, etc.

Uncontrollable and unpredictable situations happen in everyone's life, whether we like it or not. Such events develop stress (worries, anxiety, fear) and distress that adversely affect physical and mental health and well-being.

While you cannot control these external factors, but can control how you respond to them. Like a skilled captain of

the sailboat, you can adjust your sails, change course, and make the best of the conditions you encounter. By staying adaptable, resilient, and proactive,

you can navigate through life's unpredictable seas with grace and determination. The following strategies can be applied to rough and tough weather of life:

- **Focus on what you can control**: To deal with such situations, use your power of discrimination to know what situations you can, or cannot control. Take action on what you can control. Apply your strengths to overcome the problem.

- **Acceptance:** Accept the situations you cannot control. Acknowledging the reality that there will be storms, waves, cool breezes, and hot winds in life also, like in the sea. Accepting the reality of the situation can help you approach unpleasant events with a cool mind.

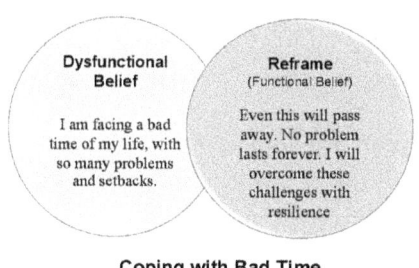

Coping with Bad Time

- **Even this will pass away:** Internalize the powerful spiritual principle - everything and every event of life is temporary. Keep in mind that *"even this will pass away"*, a powerful belief will give you spiritual strength to accept any adverse situation in life.
- **Appreciate your feelings**: Allow yourself to acknowledge and experience your emotions, whether it's frustration, sadness, or anxiety. By recognizing and accepting your emotions, you can cope with them.
- **Preparation**: Be proactive, and prepare yourself for life's challenges by acquiring appropriate knowledge, skills, and resources. In real-life situations, this might involve creating an emergency fund, building a supportive network, or developing coping mechanisms.
- **Seek support**: Take the help of family members, friends, or a therapist for support and encouragement. Talking to someone who listens without judgment can provide guidance and perspective on your situation.
- **Flexibility**: Be flexible in your approach to navigating life's ups and downs. In some situations, you may need

to revise your plans or change course entirely to adapt to changing circumstances.
- **Mindfulness**: Stay present and mindful of your thoughts, emotions, and reactions to different situations. Mindfulness can help you respond to challenges with greater clarity and composure.

By integrating these approaches, you can effectively manage the "weather" in your life and navigate towards your goals with greater resilience and confidence.

Accept your *Prarabdha*

Good or bad, what you put out comes back to you!
Law of Karma

According to Vedas, all human actions are governed by Law of Karma. There is no, flaw in Law of Karma. It is an exact and accurate regulation of actions and reactions.

"Man eats what he cooks. That is, he reaps what he sows."

(Atharva Veada 12.3.48)

Law of karma is based upon the conclusion that this life is not an end in itself but is just an incident in the eternal existence of each one of us. The chain of cause and effect is an endless, continuous event of the nature. As per this law, the man is accountable for his own deeds to the extent he has the freedom of choosing his course of action.

Based on the gathered impressions (samskaras) of the past and present actions, karma is classified into three distinct categories;

- **Sanchit Karma** (Accumulated Karma): these are the accumulated effects of the past karma that will fructify in future life or lives.
- **Prarabdha Karma** (Fructifying Karma): Prarabdha, in the context of karma, refers to the portion of your past actions that are manifesting in your current life. It's like a pre-set menu of experiences your soul chose to encounter for growth. Prarabdha is often likened to destiny or fate. It encompasses things like your physical body, family background, and certain unavoidable events of life. You can't change these core experiences, but you can choose how you react to them. Prarabdha offers the opportunity for internal growth. The challenges you face in your life journey can be opportunities to develop resilience, patience, or compassion. How you respond to these situations shapes your future karma.

  Acceptance of Prarabdha: There is no escape from prarabdha. All your thoughts, words and deeds and their consequences, happiness and sorrow are effects of your prarabdha. Resisting Prarabdha can lead to frustration and suffering. Accepting it doesn't mean resignation, but rather acknowledging what is and focusing on what you can control – your attitude, choices, and reactions. By accepting Prarabdha and focusing on your present choices, you can transform unavoidable experiences into opportunities for growth.

- **Aagami Karma** (Prospecting karma): The effects or impressions of your current thoughts, words, and deeds those are accumulating and will fructify in due course.

Some of the prarabdha karma led to certain actions, which may be good or bad, whereas balance prarabdha lead to certain experiences, which may be pleasant or painful. We can control our actions by self-effort, but have no control over the experiences caused by our prarabdha. Accept your prarabdha, as it comes-pleasant or unpleasant

> **Exercise:** Visualize one of the stormy situations in the life of your friend, who is not able to cope with it, and seeks your support. What strategy you will adopt to help him?

Step 10: Cultivate Relationships

Foster meaningful connections with those around you to enrich your journey: In the sailboat metaphor, "other boats" represent the "other people" in your life, who may be various individuals or groups involved in or affected by a particular endeavor or journey. They can either support or hinder your journey, or do not make any difference in your life, depending on their intention and how you handle them. They can influence your journey broadly in three ways; positive (supportive), negative (problematic), or neutral (indifferent). The other boats can be classified in the following types:

Positive, Neutral, & Negative People

Other Boats in Life		
Other Boats	*Description*	*How to handle them?*
Support Boats	These are individuals or groups who provide support, resources, and encouragement, to help you move forward. They may include mentors, coaches, friends, family members, or colleagues.	Handling support boats in real life involves building and nurturing relationships, seeking assistance when needed, and expressing gratitude for the support received.
Competing Boats	These represent competitors or adversaries who may be competing for similar goals. They could be rival businesses, opposing teams, or individuals with conflicting interests.	Handling competing boats in life involves understanding their strategies, strengths, and weaknesses. Focusing on your strengths and maintaining a competitive edge through innovation, or strategic positioning.
Distracting Boats	These represent individuals or factors that may divert attention or resources away from the main sailboat's goals. They could include distractions such as conflicts, rumours, or competing priorities.	Handling distracting boats in real life involves maintaining focus, setting boundaries, and prioritizing tasks and relationships that contribute positively to the journey.
Collaborative Boats	These are individuals or groups who share similar goals or interests and may collaborate with the main sailboat to achieve common objectives. They could be partners, allies, or stakeholders with complementary skills or resources.	Handling collaborative boats in real life involves promoting positive relationships, communicating effectively, and leveraging shared expertise to achieve mutual success.

Design Your Life

Advisory Boats	These are individuals or groups who offer advice, expertise, or guidance based on their experience or knowledge. They could include mentors, consultants, or experts in relevant fields	Handling advisory boats in real life involves being open to feedback, seeking out diverse perspectives, and leveraging insights to make informed decisions and navigate challenges effectively.
Neutral Boats	These are individuals or groups who remain indifferent or neutral to your activities.	Handling neutral boats in real life involves being open to developing good relationships with them.

Effective handling of "other boats" in real life requires understanding their roles, managing relationships, and navigating interactions with care and good intentions.

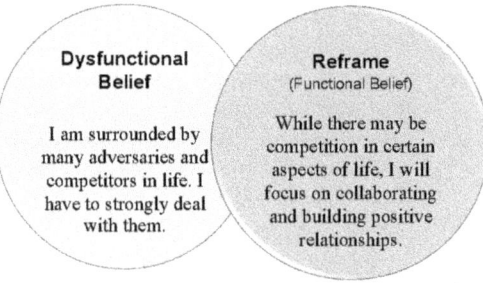

Cultivating Relationship

Exercise: Reflect on your current work and family life and try to identify and classify the people around you into positive, negative, and neutral types.

***

Chapter 11
Take Control of Your Destiny

Taking control of your destiny is about recognizing that you have the power to influence the direction of your life through your choices, actions, and mindset. It involves being proactive rather than reactive, and taking ownership of your decisions and their consequences through following steps:

- Step11: Embrace your Role: Take the responsibility as captain of your life
- Step 12: Develop and Odyssey Plan: Make an life improvement plan for next 5 years

Step 11: Embrace Your Role

Embracing this step means acknowledging that external circumstances may impact your journey, but ultimately, you hold the reins. It's about cultivating a sense of agency and autonomy, refusing to be solely dictated by fate or external forces.

By embracing your role as the architect of your own destiny, you empower yourself to "design your life" you desire. This involves setting clear goals, making strategic plans, and taking decisive action to move towards your aspirations.

However, controlling your destiny doesn't mean ignoring uncertainty or expecting everything to go according to plan. It's about adapting and learning from setbacks, persevering through challenges, and continuously adjusting your course as needed.

Ultimately, by taking charge of your destiny, you shape your own narrative and carve out a fulfilling and purposeful life aligned with your values, passions, and aspirations.

Lead by Example

As you have seen in the case studies **presented in the starting chapter,** Robin, Evengela, Rocky and Jacob had good leadership skills to attain their career goals, but they failed to attain the goals of family life, physical life and spiritual lives. For attaining success in all domains of life, holistic leadership skills are essential to support you and your team by goal setting, problem solving, motivating and engaging the team members to complete the tasks. Before leading others, you need to lead yourself and set example. Leading yourself effectively is the foundation for leading others. Here's how you can design your life to develop self-leadership, and leading others.

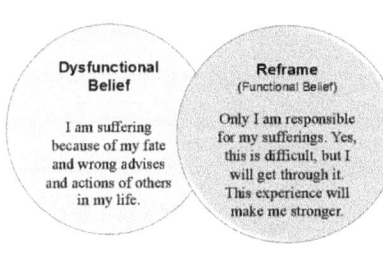

Taking Responsibilities

Self-Leadership: Leadership and "design your life" are surprisingly interconnected. Here's how:

- **Designing your life is self-leadership.** You're setting goals, making decisions, and taking action to create the future you desire. The skills you use in leading yourself are similar to the skills used in leading others.

- **Self-awareness:** Both require a deep understanding of yourself, your values, and your strengths and weaknesses. Knowing yourself allows you to set goals that align with who you are and make choices that will lead you to fulfilment.

- **Vision:** Effective leaders have a clear vision for the future. Similarly, designing your life requires you to develop a vision for your ideal life. This vision guides your decisions and motivates you to keep moving forward.

- **Decision-Making:** Leaders are constantly making choices. Designing your life involves making decisions about your career, relationships, and overall well-being. Strong decision-making skills are essential in both areas.

- **Taking Initiative:** Leaders don't wait for things to happen, they take initiative. The same is true for designing your life. You need to be proactive in pursuing your goals and creating the life you want.

Leading Others: To lead others, it is most important that you are equipped with a pure mind and clear knowledge of the purpose and process of life and organization. Design your life develops your leadership in the following ways;

- **Designing a fulfilling life can make you a better leader.** When you're happy and fulfilled, you're more likely to be positive, motivated, and resilient. These qualities are essential for inspiring and motivating others.

- **Leadership skills can benefit your personal life.** Communication, delegation, and conflict resolution skills - all crucial for leadership - can also be helpful in managing your personal relationships and achieving your goals.

- **Leading by Example:** If you're designing a life that prioritizes well-being, work-life balance, and purpose, it sets a positive example for those around you.

Step 12: Develop an Odyssey Plan

Odyssey planning is a concept developed by Stanford University's design school. It's a framework for life design for a set period of 3 -5 years. The inspiration likely comes from the classic Greek epic poem, the Odyssey, by Homer. The poem follows Odysseus on a long, adventurous journey home after the Trojan War. Similarly, an Odyssey plan helps you chart a course for your own personal journey, with goals and experiences as your destinations.

An Odyssey Plan helps you envision your life over next 5 years by exploring different scenarios. It's not about having a single, fixed destination, but considering multiple possibilities and what would make your life fulfilling. There are typically three parts:

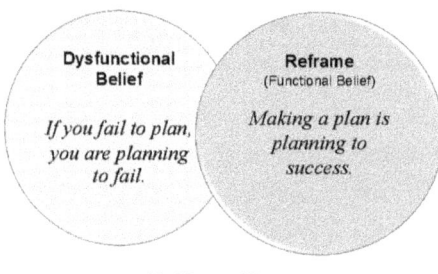

Making a Plan

1. **Current Path:** Imagine your life over 5 years if you continue on your current course. What would your physical condition, lifestyles, relationships, work, and inner peace look like?

2. **Alternative Path:** Consider a different direction. Maybe you've been thinking about a career change or moving to a new location. Explore what this path would necessitate.

3. **Dream Path:** Take constraints like money and time off the table. What would your ideal life look like? Imagine your perfect work, hobbies, and lifestyle.

By considering these different scenarios, you gain clarity on what truly matters to you and what steps you might take to get there.

How to Develop a 5-Year Odyssey Plan

1. **Choose Your Format:** There's no right or wrong way. Use a mind map, write a narrative, or create a vision board for each scenario.

2. **Brainstorm Freely:** Don't hold back on ideas. The more possibilities you explore, the richer your understanding of yourself will be.

3. **Consider the Details:** For each path, think about health, lifestyle, relationships, play, work, finances, and inner peace. What resources would you need? How would you feel?

4. **Reflect and Analyse:** Once you have explored all three paths, see if any common themes or goals emerge. Are there skills you need to develop? Is there a way to combine elements from different paths?

5. **Take Action:** Your Odyssey Plan is a springboard, not a destination. Identify small, actionable steps you can take towards your goals.

Example: Robin's Odyssey Plan

Robin is a corporate professional at an age of 40 years, working in multinational corporation. He has undergone training on DYL. To put the new learning in practice he wants to develop an odyssey plan for the next 5 years. His aspirations for improvements in four life domains are as below:

Robin has assessed his present state of life and developed a Dash Board indication his present state and goals for the next five years.

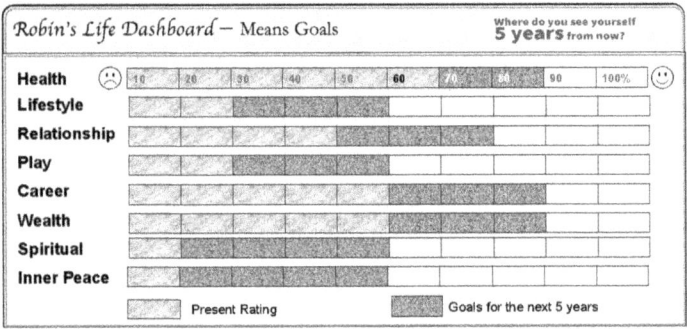

- **Physical Life:** Robin wants to improve his current health level of 60% to 80% during the next 5 years by addressing some health issues. Change life style to improve his diet, practice regular exercise and morning walk and light sports.
- **Family Life:** Robin plans to make a pleaser trip to Italy, France, and Switzerland with family during next year. Spend enough quality time with spouse, children and parents. Join a weekend music school to learn Harmonium, which he wished during early teenage. Enjoy playing musical instruments.
- **Work life:** Currently Robin is working in Business Excellence discipline of a manufacturing industry, now wants to change his job in Consulting field.

Wants to increase his earning by 80% during the next five years.

- **Spiritual Life:** Currently Robin does not have any formal exposure of concepts and practices of spirituality, but understands its importance in life. Robin wants to join a spiritual mission to learn and practice spirituality, yoga and meditation as integral part of his lifestyle.

Based on the life dash board, Robin identified the problems which will be taken up as Life Improvement projects:

Robin's DYL Projects - Next 5 Years

*	#	KPIs	Present	Goal	Gap	Projects / Problems
Physical Life	1	Health	60	80	20	Improve Health by Medical Consultation
Physical Life	2	Lifestyle	40	70	30	Change Lifestyle – Plan a Routine, Nutritious Diet, Exercise
Family Life	3	Relationships	50	80	30	Improve Relationship with family members
Family Life	4	Passion/Play	20	60	40	Make a pleasure trip to Switzerland and European countries
Work Life	5	Work/Career	50	80	30	Develop new skills- Attend courses and Look for better job
Work Life	6	Wealth Creation	50	80	30	Increase income by taking up some consulting assignments
Spiritual Life	7	Self Awareness	10	50	40	Join a spiritual mission. Take up courses on spirituality
Spiritual Life	8	Inner Peace	10	50	40	Lean and practice Patanjali Yoga and Meditation techniques

Based on the Robin's aspirations and identified improvement projects, a typical Odyssey Plan for the next 5 years is presented here:

Robin's Odyssey Plan

	Current Path (Year 1)	Alternate Path (Year-2)	Dream Path (Year 3)
Physical Life	Robin can begin by making small changes to improve his health. He can start a walking routine for 30 minutes a day and track his food intake using a mobile app.	Robin can consult a doctor to create a personalized fitness program to address his health issues. A consultation with a nutritionist can help revamp his diet for a more	In his ideal scenario, Robin achieves an 80% health level through regular exercise, a healthy diet, and stress management techniques like

		balanced approach to eating.	yoga and meditation.
Family Life	Robin can start saving for his family trip to Europe by allocating a specific amount in his budget. Researching potential destinations in Italy, France, and Switzerland and comparing deals can be a great first step.	Booking flights or accommodations in advance (if feasible) can secure better deals for Robin's family trip.	Robin embarks on a dream European vacation with his family, creating lasting memories.
Work Life	To transition into consulting, Robin can research management consulting roles and identify required skills through online courses, conferences, or attending industry events. Networking with professionals in the field can also be beneficial.	Robin can look for freelance consulting projects or part-time consulting work that leverage his experience. This will help him build a portfolio and gain experience in the consulting field.	Robin successfully transitions into a management consulting role, exceeding expectations and achieving a significant increase in his income.
Spiritual Life	Robin can begin exploring his interest in spirituality by visiting local yoga studios and meditation centres to find a practice that resonates with him. There are also many online courses and resources available for beginners.	Consider online courses or retreats focused on meditation and yoga. In addition to these practices, Robin can explore introductory texts on Eastern philosophy or spiritual traditions that pique his interest.	Robin joins a spiritual mission where he learns directly from a realized Guru and practices Patanjali Yoga. This practice helps him achieve true inner peace and integrate his spiritual learnings into his daily life.
Date:		**Age:**	

Robin's Odyssey Plan	
Integration & Growth (Year 4 & 5)	
Physical Life	**Maintain health:** Robin should continue exercising regularly and maintaining a balanced diet.
Family Life	**Nurture family:** Schedule regular family time for activities everyone enjoys.
Work Life	**Thrive in consulting:** Robin can apply his consulting skills and knowledge to make a positive impact within his new company.
Spiritual Life	**Deepen spirituality:** Robin can continue to deepen his spiritual practice through meditation retreats, attending lectures, or reading scriptures.
Key Actions for Robin:	
<ul><li>**Track progress:** Robin can use a journal, tracker app, or vision board to monitor his progress in each area.</li><li>**Develop new skills:** Robin can enroll in courses, workshops, or certifications to enhance his skillset for his desired career change.</li><li>**Seek support:** A health coach, career counsellor, or spiritual mentor can provide valuable guidance on Robin's journey.</li><li>**Embrace flexibility:** Robin should be prepared to adapt his plan as needed based on unforeseen circumstances.</li></ul>	
<ul><li>Celebrate achievements, big or small.</li><li>Don't hesitate to ask for help when needed.</li><li>Enjoy the journey - self-improvement and growth is a lifelong process.</li></ul>	
Date:	Age:

This Odyssey Plan provides a framework for Robin. He can personalize it further with specific details, milestones, and resources according to his situations.

Develop your Life Dash Board- set your goals for next 5 years, identify problems of your life that need to be solved and develop Odyssey plan using the following formats.

Design Your Life

Your Life Dashboard Means Goals.		Name:			Date			Where do you see yourself **5 years** from now?		
Health ☹	10	20	30	40	50	60	70	80	90	100% ☺
Lifestyle										
Relationship										
Play										
Career										
Wealth										
Spiritual										
Inner Peace										

Present Rating | Goals for the next 5 years

Your DYL Projects – Next 5 Years						Name: Date:
*	#	KPIs	Present	Goal	Gap	Projects / Problems
Physical Life	1	Health				
	2	Lifestyle				
Family Life	3	Relationships				
	4	Passion/Play				
Work Life	5	Work/Career				
	6	Wealth Creation				
Spiritual Life	7	Self Awareness				
	8	Inner Peace				

Odyssey Plan					
Life	Year-1	Year-2	Year-3	Year-4	Year-5
Physical					
Family					
Work					
Spiritual					
Name:			Date:		Age:

A typical example of Odyssey plan is illustrated in a case study presented in the next chapter. You can further elaborate it to provide more details of plan to put into action. Apply your creativity to make your plan with interesting graphics and visuals.

> **Exercise:** To put the DYL learning in action, Set your targets, Identify the improvement projects, Develop an Odyssey Plan for next five years and implement it from the first date of coming month.

***

Chapter 12
Steering Towards Tomorrow

Steering towards Tomorrow

Throughout this book, we have delved into the intricacies of life, uncovering its mysteries, exploring its purpose, and dissecting the elements that contribute to a well-designed life. From the metaphor of the sailboat journey to the practical steps of self-discovery, goal-setting, and navigating challenges, you have been equipped with tools to embark on a journey of personal growth and fulfilment.

After understanding the twelve steps of "Design Your Life", let us go back to life stories of Robin, Evengela, Jacob, and Rocky, presented in the first chapter of the book, and analyze, why they failed to live a truly happy life despite great success in career and wealth creation?

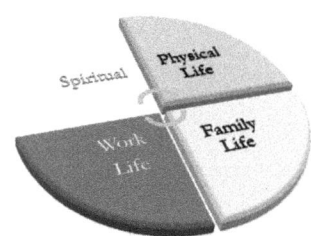
Living a Partial Life

One of the main reasons is, they lived a partial life. They focused only on work life, ignored family and physical lives, and practically spiritual life was not at all addressed. Holistic life and happiness (wellbeing) is not a partial experience. This is common situation in life of majority of the people.

To design a holistic life, Robin, Evengela, Jacob, Rocky, and including you must know your values, your present state of life, direction and destination of life, your weaknesses, which are hindering your progress, and essential strengths which you must acquire to accomplish your goals. Identify and solve problems of your life, and ensure that you are staying on the right path. Develop capability to cope with unpleasant events of life and cultivate relationships with people around you. Had they followed the DYL steps, they would have lived a holistic and happy life.

Design Your Life is just the beginning of your new journey. Life is dynamic and ever-changing, and as such, the process of designing and redesigning your life is ongoing. So, to steer your life towards a happy and successful tomorrow, put the DYL concepts into life in the following ways:

- **Embrace a Designer Mindset:** View yourself as the designer of your life. Proactively shape your experiences by understanding your values and goals.

- **Start with Self-Discovery:** Identify your values, strengths, and weaknesses. Self-discovery is not a one-time event but a lifelong journey. Make it a habit to check in with yourself regularly, reassessing your values, strengths, and aspirations. This will help you determine what is important to you and what kind of life you want to design.

- **Set Goals and Direction:** Once you know what you want, set goals and a clear direction for your life. Life is dynamic, and so are your dreams and ambitions. As you evolve, so too will your goals. Take the time to reassess what matters most to you and recalibrate your direction accordingly. This will give you a roadmap to follow and help you stay motivated.

- **Develop an Odyssey Plan:** Make a plan for next 5 years, break down your goals into smaller, actionable steps. After achieving your five-year plan, make the next five year plan, and so on.

- **Take Action:** Don't wait for the perfect time to start. Take action and start making progress on your goals, even if it is in small steps.

- **Stay Aligned:** Regularly assess your progress and make sure you are still on track. Be willing to adjust your course as needed.

- **Embrace Challenges:** There will be obstacles along the way. But view them as challenges to be overcome, not roadblocks. Embrace challenges as opportunities for growth. Challenges are inevitable, but they also present opportunities for learning and development. Approach them with resilience and a growth mindset, knowing that each obstacle you overcome strengthens you and propels you forward on your journey

- **Cultivate Relationships:** Build strong relationships with supportive people who will help you on your journey. Surround yourself with people who uplift and support you, and be there for them in return. Nurture connections that nourish your soul and enrich your life. Remember, we are not meant to journey alone, and the bonds we forge along the way can sustain us through life's ups and downs.

- **Find a Mentor or Coach:** A mentor or coach can provide you with guidance and support as you work to design your life.

- **Celebrate Your Successes:** Take time to celebrate your accomplishments, big and small. This will help you stay motivated and on track.

- **Never Give Up:** Designing your life is a journey, not a destination. There will be setbacks along the way, but don't give up on your dreams.

Lastly, take ownership of your destiny. You are the author of your life story, and you have the power to shape its narrative. Seize each moment with intention and purpose, knowing that every choice you make has the potential to shape your future.

To illustrate the DYL implementation approach, a brief case study is presented here.

Case Study
How to put DYL into practice?
Have you ever felt like you're on autopilot in your own life? You may have achieved a certain level of success, but something feels off. This was the case for Adam, a corporate manager who had climbed the corporate ladder and secured a good salary. Yet, he felt unfulfilled and stressed.

After attaining the DYL training, Adam realized he had been living his life "by default." It was time to take charge and steer his life in a more meaningful direction "by design".

DYL uses a sailboat metaphor to illustrate the importance of setting goals and taking action. Adam adapted this method to create his own personal roadmap, which is depicted in the following figure.

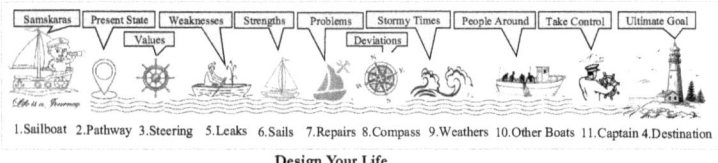
Design Your Life

The practical approach adopted by Adam to implement 12 steps of DYL are briefly explained here:

1. Who am I?

Samskaras: The design your life process begins with self-discovery, that originates from your **samskara.** Samskaras (संस्कार) are the subtle impressions of innate tendencies of a person from their past karma, that determines the true identity of a person. Like a sailboat performs the journey in the sea to reach its desired destination, Adam is going to perform the journey of life through his physical existence in the physical world to attain his goals of life. Adam's true identity is not his name, designation physical shape and size, social status, and wealth created, but what are his core values, which are shaped by the samskaras with which he is born.

As explained in step-1 of the DYL technique, when Adam did introspection and analysed his samskaras for the first time in his life. He discovered that his values are highly influenced by his materialistic thinking, personal ego, perfectionism, judgmental and critical nature from his samskaras. His negative samskaras influenced in shaping many negative values in his behaviour resulting in unhappiness and unfulfillment. Had he or his parents discovered such negative samskaras, at the early stages of life, they could have taken some measures to transcend them to positive samskaras. The outcome of this step is to identify the negative samskaras, which must be transcended to positive.

2. Where am I on pathway of my life?

Present State: The water of the sea is the pathway of a sailboat journey. Similarly, according to the natural design of the creator, Adam has to perform his life journey on four natural pathways (domains); physical life, family life, work life, and spiritual life. Adam is on a life journey, unless he knows where he is at this moment on his life pathway, he can't know the direction and determine the destination of his life. The four domains of life are further divided into 8 key performance indicators; health, lifestyle, relationships, play/passion, career/work, wealth creation, self-awareness, and inner peace.

The step-2 involves the self-assessment of the present state of the four pathways of life, in a quantified way, so that it can be quantitatively measured, monitored, and improved. The present state is the baseline assessment of life. Based on personal standards, Adam self-assessed that on the physical pathway, his score is 50%, family pathway 60%, work or career pathway 80%, and spiritual pathway 5%. These data are presented on a life dashboard, indicating the present state, and gap between the desired and present state, and imbalance in his life, which must be addressed by "design your life" to attain the goals of life.

3. Is my life going in right direction?

Values: Values are the fundamental beliefs that guide our lives and determine our decisions and direction of life like the steering of the sailboat. Values shape who we are, how we make decisions, and how we interact with the world around us. Every person is unique and holds a set of personal values. Personal values are the unique beliefs you hold about what's right and wrong. They influence everything from your self-esteem to your relationships. Examples include; honesty, kindness, compassion, and adventure.

Till now, Adam was not aware of his values, but his values are the core of his personality and driving his life. Values may be positive or negative and accordingly, they take you in the right and wrong direction.

The purpose of the step-3 activity of DYL is to identify the wrong values governing your life, so that you can change them to positive values. But how to decide what is wrong or right? This is clarified by the Lord of death- Yama Raj, in a famous scripture Kath Upanishad, with the concept of Preyas (pleasant but not good for you) and Shreyas (the good for you). Adam recognized that he is driven by mostly Preyas values, due to ignorance. Changing the negative value to positive is the core activity of DYL. Spiritual concepts and psychological techniques like NLP (Neuro Linguistic Programming) are used to change the values. The outcome of this step is to identify the negative values you must change to improve your life.

4. What is destination of my life?

Goals of life: Like the sailboat has a specific destination as its goal of the journey, similarly the destination of Adam's life is defined as the goals of life. There are two types of goals; end goals and means goals. The end goal or ultimate purpose of life – Happiness. Everyone is in search of happiness only, irrespective of his position, status, culture, or religion. But happiness is not an object, it is a unique experience that can be achieved through four types of means goals of physical, family, work, and spiritual lives.

The outcome of this activity of DYL is setting the means goals of physical, family, work, and spiritual lives and displaying them on the life dashboard as done in step 2. Short-term goals of life are set by Adam for the next five years quantitatively as % value on life dashboard. Adam has set goals to be achieved during the next 5 years as: physical life 80%, family life 80%, work-life 90%, and spiritual life 50%. An action plan developed by Adam to achieve the means goals.

5. What is hindering progress of my life?

Personal Weaknesses: Everyone has weaknesses. Personal weaknesses in your life as the leaks of the sailboat hinder progress in your life. The key is to identify them, work on improvement, and focus on your strengths to keep moving forward. The weaknesses in your physical, psychological, intellectual, and spiritual aspects of personality are reflected in your behaviour and can drain your mental energy making it harder to focus and take action to move forward.

Adam recognized that leaks of his personality in the form of imperfect behaviour are affecting his health, relationships, performance at the workplace, promotions, wealth-creating capabilities, success, happiness, and inner peace.

Just like water seeping in the boat reduces ability of the sailboat to stay afloat and make headway, leaks in your behaviour can be a source of constant worry and stress. This can cloud your judgment and make it difficult to make good decisions, hindering your progress. The outcome of the step 4 activity performed by Adam figured out his weaknesses in all four domains of his personality.

This is like finding the source of the leak in the boat. Once you know your weaknesses, you can work on mending them. This could involve learning new skills, setting boundaries, or seeking help. It's like fixing the leak in the boat, making it seaworthy again.

6. How can I improve progress of my life?

Personal Strengths: The sailboat is equipped with a set of sails that harness the power of the wind to move it forward in the right direction toward the destination. Similarly, your physical body, mind, intellect, and spirit are sails of your lifeboat which are used to tap the energy of your physical, psychological, intellectual, and spiritual resources to move toward your life goals. Your desires, aspirations, motivation, and enthusiasm work as the wind- the propelling force, which depends on the strength of your health, relationships, attitude, emotions, knowledge, skills, inner peace, faith, and self-confidence. Personal strengths are the most important factor in attaining success, happiness, and fulfilment in life.

Realizing the importance of personal strengths, Adam, identified what knowledge, skills, and attitude he needs to attain his life goals in all four domains of physical, family, work, and spiritual lives. After identification Adam made an action plan to develop his competence in desired areas. There are several approaches available to improve personal strengths such as; lifestyle change, positive psychology, professional competence related to work, problem-solving skills, spiritual practices, etc. Finally, Adam took the initiative to learn and practice his physical, psychological, intellectual, and spiritual strengths.

7. What are the current problems of my life?

Problems are facts of life, there can't be a problem-free world. Actually, problem is not the problem, the attitude towards the problem is problem. Problems are opportunities for improvement. Instead of worrying about the problem, it is important to learn the problem-solving techniques and solve the problem. Design thinking has evolved as one of the most effective human-centered problem-solving techniques that can be used to solve problems of life also, in addition to solving problems of products, services, and processes.

According to DYL step 7, Adam reflected on all areas of his life and recognized and identified the problems in four domains of his life. Made a comprehensive list of all the problems in his life, and prioritized them based on importance and urgency. Adam took action to solve each problem using a design thinking framework.

8. Is my life going on the right track?

Deviations: In the sailboat journey, to ensure that it is moving in the right direction, the captain uses a compass to find any deviation from the planned route. If any deviation is observed corrective actions is taken to stay aligned. Similarly, to ensure that your life is moving on the right track according to design, you have to use our mental compass. If any deviation is taking place from your life plan, it is expressed by your mind in form of negative emotions, unhappiness, or gut feelings.

If any such deviations are felt, it is analyzed and appropriate action is taken to stay aligned with the life design. Adam was sensitive to his mental signals and took appropriate corrective action as and when required to move according to plan.

9. How to manage the stormy situations of life?

Stormy Time: The sailboat, during its journey faces several stormy weathers, strong wind, and turbulent waves, to navigate under such situations requires competence, confidence and navigating skills. Similarly, in the journey of life, no one can have only pleasant situations all the time. Everyone faces stormy or unpleasant times also along with happy moments, success and failures both are part of life.

To cope with stormy moments in life is a big challenge, especially in situations like; loss of loved ones, break-ups in relationships, heavy loss in business, loss of job, failing to get promotions, serious disease, defeat in competitions, unpleasant events, etc.

Some people, who are psychologically and spiritually weak, are not able to face such situations and get depressed or mentally disturbed. On the extreme some people develop addiction of drug or alcohol to cope with setbacks. To navigate stormy weather requires developing the inner strength and adaptability to face adversity with courage, perseverance, and a positive mindset.

Adam also faced such situations in life, which he could cope with adapting spiritual practices and a positive psychological technique.

1o. How to handle people around me?

The people around: A sailboat is not sailing alone, there are several sailboats around it on the same pathway. Some boats are supportive, some or competing or obstructing and most of them are indifferent. Similarly in life journey, whether it is family life or work life, everyone is surrounded by other people. Some people may be supportive, few may be against you or competing in life, and many may be neutral. To live a good and happy life, one should cultivate good relationship with everyone, even with people who are against you.

Positive psychology and spiritual transformation can develop a mindset of gratitude, forgiveness, compassion, and acceptance to manage people around you.

11. How to live a life by design?

Take Control: Finally, it is your life, so for you were living life "by default"-which was controlled by external circumstances. But after going through the above 10 steps, now you are going to live life "by design". Take control of your life by following the DYL steps.

Adam has taken control of his life by clearly figuring out his values, which are the real guiding factor of his life.

12. How to put DYL into practice?

Odyssey Plan: After understanding the DYL framework, now it is time to start living life according to own design. To put DYL in practice, Adam developed a comprehensive Odyssey plan for the next 5 years of his life:

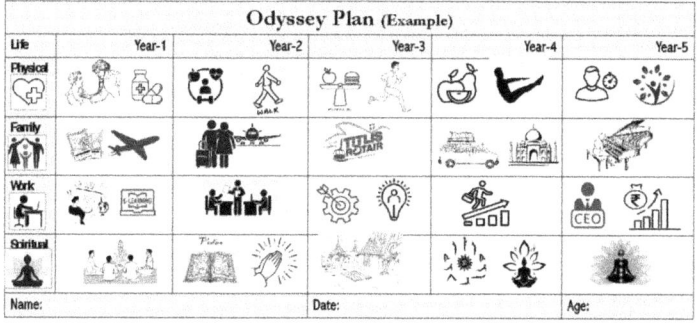

As shown in the above graphical plan, Adam designed his life to implement following activities in four domains of his life:

Physical Life: To attain his health improvement goals during the five years, Adam planned to go for a comprehensive health checkup to find out abnormalities in his health and take proper treatment to restore normal health. He changed his lifestyle by switching over to nutritious diet, daily morning walks, physical exercise, following a time discipline for waking up, exercise, work, meals, and sleep. Regular practice of yoga and naturopathy practices.

Family Life: To attain the family life goals during the five years, Adam planned a pleasure trip with his family to famous tourist places of Europe, especially a visit to beautiful glacier covered mountains of Switzerland. He started to find the right travel agency, interesting itinerary to book the trip. Made yearly plan to visit the tourist places of India. To pursue his childhood passion for music, Adam planned to learn and play piano and other musical instruments and joined a music academy.

Work-Life: To attain his work-life goals, Adam planned to enhance his competency related to his functional role, problem-solving skills, continuous improvement techniques, leadership skills, and behavioral skills. He decided to take up e-learning courses and attend training programs to learn new techniques. He planned to take initiatives at his workplace to make improvements in the processes, people, and culture of his employer organization. He planned to attain career progress and wealth-creating capabilities by improving his competence, engagement, and performance.

Spiritual Life: During the self-assessment at step 2, Adam discovered that his performance in the spiritual life is practically negligible. Realizing its importance for fulfilment and happiness in life, Adam made a plan to attain an ambitious goal for spiritual transformation. He planned to join a well-respected spiritual organization to learn the basic concepts of spirituality, followed by self-study of scriptures through correspondence courses and attending classes in spiritual ashrams. He started learning a practicing yoga and meditation and made it an essential part of his new lifestyle. By regular practice of spirituality, he will be able to transform his materialistic thinking into spirituality, which will result in enhancement in his inner peace and happiness.

By following the above steps, Adam was able to take control of his life and find greater fulfilment. This case study shows that it's never too late to take charge and create a life you love. Is it time for you to chart your own course?

As you close the final pages of "Design Your Life," remember that the canvas of your life is yours to paint. Embrace the journey with courage, curiosity, and an unwavering belief in your ability to create the life you desire. Your adventure awaits- chart your course, set sails, and steer your life towards a happier tomorrow.

> **Exercise:** Make an Odyssey Plan for the next 5 years of your life.

***

Acknowledgments

Writing a book on the complex subject of "design your life" is a humbling undertaking. Witnessing the current environment and lifestyles of people, especially the younger generation, propelled me to share the experiences I have gained during my seven-decades of life journey. My education, profession, and upbringing have given me a well-rounded perspective, exposing me to modern technology, positive psychology, and spirituality. These multifaceted experiences, and study of Vedantic scriptures, inspired me to synergize Eastern and Western wisdom into a holistic concept of Design Your Life.

Weaving spirituality into the fabric of my life has been a deeply enriching experience. Since 1980, I have been fortunate to pursue the study and practice of spirituality under the guidance of esteemed Gurus of Chinmaya Mission, Art of Living, Isha Yoga, and Yogoda Satsang Society. I am immensely grateful to these enlightened Gurus for introducing me to life-changing practices of Transcendental Meditation, Patanjali Yoga, Sudarshan Kriya, Inner Engineering, and Kriya Yoga.

I have used some graphics from the Google clipart sources to provide visual expression of contents, I am grateful to original designers with due credit to their copyrights and creativity.

I am grateful to Dr. Girdhar Gyani, Director General AHPI, a renowned global quality expert, for expressing his views about the book in form of foreword.

I am indebted to the positive psychology experts, particularly the Martin Seligman, Hugo Alberts and Seph Fontane and design thinking experts Bill Burnett and Dave Evans of

Acknowledgments

Stanford University, whose published work has been a great source of inspiration.

I am forever grateful to my parents and elder brother for planting the seeds of spirituality in my early years. Their influence instilled a deep curiosity and a lifelong quest for spiritual growth within me.

Words cannot express my appreciation for the unwavering support and encouragement I received from my family throughout the writing of this book. I am especially indebted to my wife Pushpa and my children; Aalok, Archana, Avinash, Ritu, Siddharth, Avni, and Shivoham for their love and support.

My sincere thanks go out to the Blue Rose publishers and team, for their efforts in designing, printing, distribution, and making this book available to a wider audience.

Finally, and most importantly, I am deeply grateful to each reader who picks up this book. My hope is that it will serve as a guiding light on their journey to a more fulfilling life. I eagerly welcome reader's feedback, both positive and constructive, as it will help me refine the knowledge presented in this book and better serve future readers. (ansingh11@gmail.com)

Akhilesh N Singh

About the Author

Akhilesh N Singh is a Design Your Life Coach, Management Consultant, Spiritual Seeker, NLP Practitioner, Academician, Corporate Trainer, and Author. He brings a unique blend of professional expertise and spiritual wisdom to his work.

A Spiritual Seeker: Along with his professional responsibilities, since 1980, Akhilesh Singh has been dedicated to learning and practicing spirituality. He has formally studied Vedanta scriptures including Upanishads, Yoga Sutra, Brahma Sutra, Yoga Vasishta, Bhagavad Gita, and Vedic Jyotish. He learned techniques of Transcendental Meditation, Patanjali Yoga, Sudarshan Kriya, Inner Engineering, and Kriya Yoga from enlightened Gurus of Chinmaya Mission, Art of Living, Isha Yoga, and Yogoda Satsang Society in ashrams located on Himalayan Mountains and several other serene places.

Management Consultant: Having over five decades of industrial, academic and management consulting experience. He is a specialist of Lean, Six Sigma, and TQM. Trained in Toyota Motor Corporation & Kaizen Institute Japan, Lean Enterprise Academy UK, and Armco Inc. USA. Six Sigma Black Belt from

ASQ. He has extensive consulting and training experiences of working with leading organizations in India, Bangladesh, Saudi Arabia, Qatar, and UAE. Worked in Steel Authority of India, Jindal Stainless Ltd, FICCI and UNIDO.

Educator & Author: Akhilesh Singh worked as a Professor at Asia Pacific Institute of Management, New Delhi, and Corporate trainer. He has authored 17 books, including ***Design Your Life***, Enhancing Global Competitiveness of Steel, Spiritual Intelligence, Radical Cost Reduction, Goal of all goals of Life, Zero Defect Zero Effect, Lean Manufacturing, Lean IT, Quality Audit, Creating Customer Driven Quality, Quality System Documentation, Quality Guide, ISO Quality Management System, and Stainless Steel.

Education: B. Tech from IIT- BHU Varanasi (Yr.1972) with postgraduate in Management and Gembakaizen (Japan). Studied and qualified courses in Vedanta, Vedic Astrology, and Neuro Linguistic Programming.

"Design Your Life" Coach: To promote DYL concept of design thinking, positive psychology, and practical spirituality, and facilitate professionals to improve quality of life, offering a unique two-day in-house workshop for corporate organizations. The objective of workshop is to develop hands-on skill of participants on how to "Design Your Life" to attain success and happiness in physical, family, work, and spiritual lives.

***

Design Your Life
Two-day In-house Workshop

The key to success of business revolves around focusing not only on customers, but now equally on employees. Happiness of employees makes a difference to business of the organization. Happy employees feel pride in their work, and

they like what they do. Happy people get self-inspired, creatively engage themselves to deliver their best performance with higher job satisfaction.

Design Your Life improves the job-satisfaction of employees and organization culture. The people living life "by default" are unable to control their performance at work place and in personal life. By learning to live life "by design", people can improve their performance at workplace and in personal lives. "Design Your Life" workshop develops skill of participants to design and live a life of their aspirations, using three powerful concepts:

- **Positive Psychology**- Understanding the science of happiness and designing a life based on sailboat metaphor to live a successful and fulfilling life.

- **Practical Spirituality**- Applying spiritual concepts to attain inner peace by spiritual transformation.

- **Design Thinking-** Learning a human-centered problem-solving technique to solve problems of personal life and work life.

What participants will learn?

Participants will get clear understanding of fundamental aspects of life and develop skill to design their life:

- What is life?
- What is the purpose of life?
- How to attain the purpose of Life?
- How to design life to accomplish the purpose?

Design Your Life: Course Outline	
Day1: Demystifying Life	**Day2: Designing Life**
1. Introduction: Present state of life of the people	**6. Set Direction & Destination of Life:** Identify your Values and Set Life Goals
2. Demystifying Life: Psycho- Spiritual views of Life and its purpose	**7. Address Your Weaknesses & Strengths:** Identify your Weaknesses and Develop right Skills for success in life.
3. Sailboat Metaphor: Life is like a Sailboat Journey-a Positive Psychology approach.	**8. Resolve Challenges & Stay Aligned:** Problem solving using Design Thinking and Staying on track
4. Design Your Life: Psycho-Spiritual and Design Thinking to live a holistic life.	**9. Navigate Weathers & Cultivate Relationships:** Cope with bad Weather & Harmonize with people
5. Self-Discovery: Discover your true Identity & Assess your present state of life.	**10.Take Control of Your Destiny:** Embrace journey, Develop an Odyssey plan
For further information: Please Contact ansingh11@gmail.com**,** Phone: 9811054753	

Design Your Life

Books by Akhilesh N Singh

www.ingramcontent.com/pod-product-compliance
Lightning Source LLC
LaVergne TN
LVHW061611070526
838199LV00078B/7239